Marcus Field & Mark Irving

LOFTS

GINGKO PRESS

Contents

Introduction:

Loft living – the making of domestic space in buildings originally constructed for industrial use – began as a subversive act. Today, with lofts largely the preserve of a bourgeois elite and the subject of attention by architects and designers the world over, it is hard to imagine the conditions endured and the ideals held by the early pioneers of the lifestyle.

This book sets out to plot the history of the loft movement, from the spaces occupied by the first loft dwellers to the often highly architectural interiors of today. Its remit is not to be comprehensive, but to show carefully selected examples, and to let the people who have designed or lived in these spaces tell their story.

Loft living begins with the poor artists who occupied former industrial buildings in 1950s New York. The main attraction was that the spaces these buildings offered were cheap enough to rent and sizeable enough in which to both live and work. This home-cum-studio – little more than a squat with few, if any, facilities – is the origin of the modern loft. But as the research in this book suggests, precedents for the free, open-plan living space of the loft can also be located in the ideals of the Modern Movement and in the purpose-built ateliers used by European artists at the turn of the century. Apart from the space and economy that attracted artists to lofts, a number of other factors conspired to fuel the movement. In the case of New York, where the first officially recognized lofts are recorded, the phenomenon can be traced back to the social and economic changes in the SoHo district of the city. The area has become known for its heavy concentration of

cast-iron framed buildings, the earliest of which date back as far as 1850. The construction method was devised to create buildings of multiple storeys with large open-plan floorplates – ideal for light-industrial manufacturing processes. In addition, the use of cast-iron frames began to free the façade from its traditional load-bearing function, allowing large expanses of glass to fill entire spaces between columns. These buildings are now credited for their highly innovative technical, structural and architectural achievements, anticipating the dictates of modernism.

By the 1950s, many of these buildings were being abandoned by the small manufacturers whose services were either outmoded, or who were looking for more modern premises in which to work. As a result, landlords were keen to rent out their empty buildings to the artists who were so eager to move in.

As the district changed, the New York City Planning Commission also had ideas about how SoHo might be developed. One of the proposals was to demolish a series of entire blocks to make way for a new expressway. To help the Commission make its decision, Professor Chester Rapkin was engaged to make a study of the economic activity and physical condition of the district. The Rapkin Report, published in 1963, was instrumental in the saving of SoHo and for the future of the loft movement. It not only reported the remaining economic activity in the area – which it said was beneficial to the city – but also recorded the early signs of regeneration brought about by artists moving in. It also highlighted the plight of the cast-iron framed buildings to conservationists and a preservation campaign soon followed.

1 The workshop of Moe Levy & Co. in 1911. This four-storey building complex on the corner of Baxter and Walker Streets in New York contained both the factory that made the clothes and the store in which they were sold. Hard conditions are eloquently described in this photograph: in the words of one writer: 'Hours were frightfully long and irregular; starvation wages were paid [and] the places in which the worker toiled were filthy and unsanitary...'. (From *New York Life at the Turn of the Century in Photographs* by Joseph Byron, Dover, 1985.)

2 The exterior of Moe Levy & Co. in midtown Manhattan, the garment district. Although the building contains a light-manufacturing business, the tiered windows, rising up the front elevation, have been styled to resemble a Genoese or Venetian palace more than a factory.

3 Warehouses were where the country could meet the town, as in these bales of wool, which have arrived from England's West Country to be counted at the London Docks in 1946.

It didn't take long for the ideas of the loft movement to penetrate other recognized cultural centres. In Berlin and London, where ideas for improving the cities by building wide roads and high-rise housing threatened to destroy warehouses and industrial buildings, campaigns were mounted to save these structures by occupying them as homes.

But for these early loft dwellers – usually students, artists, writers or academics – the appeal was about more than economics or conservation. It was also political. By the 1950s the international middle-class suburban ideal of house and garden was firmly established. This, along with a car and a family, became the symbol of success. So to move into a decaying industrial space signified a determined opposition to the mainstream. As well as the very different type of living space offered by a loft, there was an added element of dissent: occupying industrial buildings for residential purposes was still largely illegal. The pioneers of loft living were therefore not only subversive in the way they lived, but also because they broke the law.

So how did loft living develop from a small, illegal movement in key cities like Berlin, London and New York, to the diverse, international movement of today? As suggested in chapter six, much of this is down to representations of loft living in the media. Right from the early days, loft dwellers (many of them celebrity artists) have been photographed and interviewed for magazines and newspapers. We have seen lofts on television and in the movies. Since the 1960s, architects have used lofts as sites for experiment, attracting further media attention and thus disseminating the idea of loft living as the creative lifestyle par excellence.

From their gritty origins in the 1950s, lofts have now become one of the most diverse but contested international buildings types. Developers in almost every city with a stock of run-down industrial buildings – Barcelona, Berlin, Chicago, Glasgow, Manchester, New Orleans and Paris are among them – have begun converting buildings commercially and selling spaces as shell units. The criteria for what constitutes a loft, as reflected in this book, have now been stretched to include conversions of post-war concrete-framed buildings as well as former schools and offices. As chapter seven suggests, the legacy of the loft movement has had a broad impact on other building types. The design of art galleries, shops, bars and even houses are now often informed by the culture of lofts.

Although the original ideal of loft living – maximum space at minimum cost – has often been compromised by developers in recent years, the principal of having the freedom to make your home whatever you want it to be still makes the concept highly seductive. For this reason it is not surprising to find that loft culture is still growing: this book includes examples of recent loft developments in Barcelona, Helsinki, Milan, Paris and São Paulo – all cities in which the loft movement is still young.

Ultimately, lofts are about accommodating diverse attitudes to domestic space. This book attempts to provide a history and critique of that diversity, as well as a rich visual record of one of the late twentieth-century's most intriguing building types.

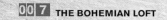

The bohemian loft

Photograph © by Fred W. McDarrah

1

Lofts have become such a staple ingredient in the way urban living has been idealized through the media of film and advertising that the early history of the phenomenon of warehouse living is easily overlooked. Loft living is primarily an American creation, developed and exported across the world: more specifically, it started in New York City, and was more an accident of economic misfortune and pragmatic individual needs than the consequence of any ideologically driven war of architectural styles.

In the area of Manhattan between the skyscrapers of midtown and the financial district of Wall Street there remained, during the early 1940s, a belt of former warehouse buildings – themselves constructed in the mid- to late-nineteenth century – that had fallen into disrepair or disuse as the once numerous light-manufacturing businesses (clothing, polishing, laundry and furniture, among many others) began to shut up shop in the face of declining sales and changing industrial practices at home and abroad. These magnificent buildings, palaces to commerce, had neither the fashionable allure of uptown nor the working dimensions or reassuring collegiate appeal of the burgeoning skyscrapers of Wall Street. However, they had two main advantages that would redefine the shape of the property market in New York City and ultimately spawn the translation of a style of living to much of the rest of the Western world. These former industrial buildings were cheap to rent and situated between two of the richest sectors of the city.

The first people to explore the neglected potential of these buildings were a small group of artists, desperate to find somewhere large and sufficiently well lit for them to live and work. In

1 Leo Castelli, a prominent New York art dealer, moved his gallery into a former industrial space to house the large-scale artworks that were being produced in the fifties and sixties.

2 Loft of the then architecture student, Leslie Gill from 1978, in New York's Greene Street. Making the most of her cast-iron columns, Gill hung coloured hammocks from them, forest-like. Other large objects – that did little to fill the huge space – were a table-tennis table, a bike, a ladder and a huge television set on feet.

2

their minds, there was the inspirational model of those artists living and working in Paris at the end of the nineteenth century, who lived, *La Bohème*-style, in the various ateliers, attics and garetts dispersed around Montmartre. Barnett Newman looked for a loft in the late 1940s, and in 1953, Robert Rauschenberg moved into one on Fulton Street, in downtown Manhattan. A writer who visited him there described the space as 'a big attic with 20-foot ceilings but no heat or running water; the rent was $15 a month, but he talked the landlord into letting him have it for $10. A hose and bucket in the back yard served as his basin, and he bathed in friends' apartments, sometimes surreptitiously, asking to use the bathroom and taking a lightning shower at the same time'.[1] Artists Jim Rosenquist and Jasper Johns also moved into disused industrial spaces, along with the iconoclastic Fluxus artists like Maciunas, Paik, Flynt

and La Monte Young, and avant-garde dancers such as Paxton, Hainer, Childs and Forti following suit over a ten-year period from 1957 to 1967. 'Fluxhouse Number 2', a leading art project initiated by the Fluxus artists, grew out of a set of housing co-ops that were based in converted lofts. SoHo itself soon developed a reputation as the centre of an innovative community of artists, with various lofts even serving as venues for performance works themselves, with the Berthold Brecht happenings at the Reuben Gallery, and Yoko Ono's performance art in her Chambers Street loft. These events – held away from the smart museums and the dealers' chic galleries – represented a radical shift in the public's understanding of what constituted an artwork, as well as questioning the appropriate setting in which an artwork could be exhibited. Susan Sontag noted that these loft-based performance

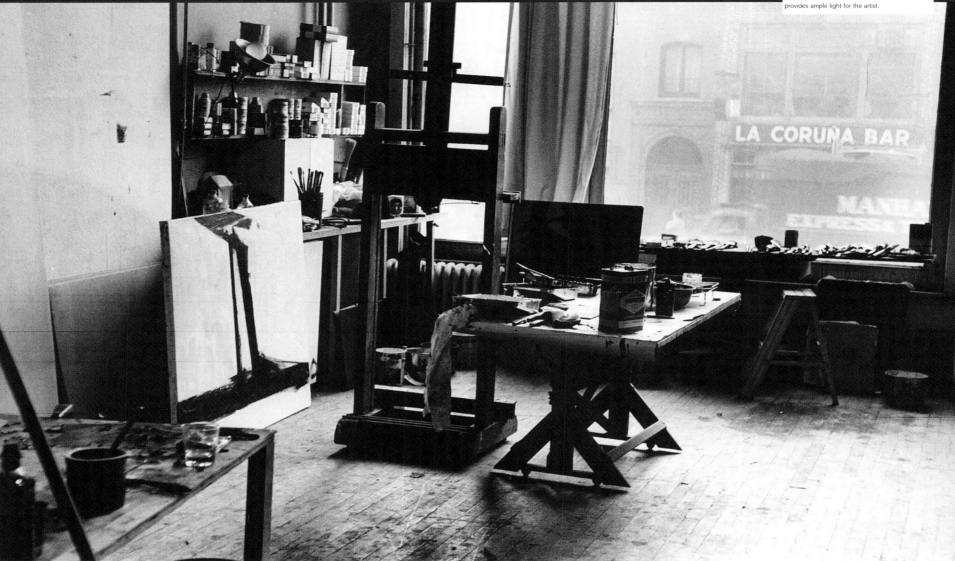

Photograph © by Fred W. McDarrah

3

events were 'not part of something bigger and fancier. And the fancy people didn't like [them], because it was all cheap and simple, and nobody could make much money out of it'.[2]

Much loft living at this time was illegal: it was only in 1964 that a law was passed that permitted an artist to occupy two floors of an abandoned factory, as long as he or she registered their details with the local authorities. Within a year of its inception, there were 3,000 registered artists in the SoHo area.[3] Artists had to place A.I.R. (Artists in Residence) plaques on their doors so that firemen would know where to go in case of a fire. These plaques have now become sought-after collectors' items.

It was not long before the dealers – who would soon take a keen interest in the work of these artists, and eventually promote them to international stardom – began to consider whether they too should take advantage of these large spaces. Betty Parsons' art gallery in the 1940s was probably the first art space to have the look and feel of an artist's loft.[4] But the exodus from the smart boutique areas of midtown, between 52nd and 77th Street, to Greenwich Village, SoHo and Tribeca took place between 1968 and 1972, with the opening of several important galleries, including those run by Paula Cooper, Richard Feigen and Leo Castelli. These relocations were motivated by more than just an interest on the part of the dealers in finding more exhibition space for less money: they also brought the dealers geographically closer to the very people who produced the items they sold, a neighbourly proximity that could only enhance their efforts to promote a new style of art production. Furthermore, the art that the artists were producing was of a size and style that looked out of place when displayed inside small galleries decorated to resemble the well-furnished apartments of their rich clients. These new works were larger, rougher and, in the case of the various Pop artists who were emerging at this time, took their inspiration from the signs of the street and from popular culture in general.

Abstract Expressionism and Pop Art are essentially American products, and it is somewhat

Photograph © by Fred W. McDarrah

4

fitting that it was in the very husks of the nation's former industrial sector that a new aesthetic vigour – one that marked the ascendancy of New York over Paris as the Western world's art capital – was to be nurtured. It is hard to know how much the environs of the loft space can be held responsible for the change in perception, evident in the 1950s and 1960s, of art as not so much something with which to decorate a space, but rather of art as an autonomous object, with an integrity unhindered by the trappings of bourgeois life. But it is undeniable that these loft spaces, with their raw cast-iron columns, stripped floors and huge internal wildernesses, provided a conveniently dynamic context against which the energy of the pioneering artists could be measured under the public gaze. These artists were, therefore, creating work within spaces which resonated with the echo of real manual labour. The photographs of the artists in their lofts show how essential to the public's understanding was their muscular, almost choreo-graphic engagement with paint and materials. The loft space and the artist are seen as one and

the same. It was inevitable, then, that the art dealers sought to recreate these loft spaces – and this is true of London's Shoreditch and Berlin's Kreuzberg districts – as art galleries and cash in on this intimate encounter with what had originally been an artist's space. Conversely, it must also be true that the phenomenon of loft living has played a vital role in domesticating the industrial aesthetic, making its features and textures acceptable to a public for whom they would have had no relevance only a few decades previously.[5]

NOTES

1 _ Sharon Zukin, *Loft Living: Culture and Capital in Urban Change* (Rutgers University Press, 1989) p. 61.

2 _ Zukin, *op. cit.* p. 94.

3 _ *American Lofts,* Lotus International 66 (Electa 1990) p. 9.

4 _ Zukin, *op. cit.* p. 95.

5 _ *American Lofts, op. cit.* p. 21.

5 (From left to right) Fufu Smith, Andy Warhol, Gerard Malanga (behind camera) and John Wilcock on the set of *Camp* at the Factory, 231 East 47th Street. In the background an elaborate arrangement of pipes have been left to provide an almost sculptural feature in the loft.

6 Elaine de Kooning, April 1961, shown painting in the loft she shared with her artist-husband, Willem.

5

Photograph © by Fred W. McDarrah

1 Lowell Nesbitt's loft was situated inside a three-storey warehouse, dating from the 1850s, close to the waterfront in Greenwich Village, New York. Its last incarnation had been as a police stables, but architect Edward E. Knowles has transformed it into a 1,670-square-metre (18,000-square-foot) loft space.

Greenwich Village, New York

Lowell Nesbitt Loft

Architecture
by Edward E. Knowles

Interior Design
by Mara Palmer

Situated in a former three-storey police stables – the building was originally constructed in the 1850s – the home and studio of the late artist Lowell Nesbitt is an early example of a unique kind of Greenwich Village loft, which has all but disappeared. Converted by Edward E. Knowles in the early-seventies, Nesbitt's loft was an example of how the loft space enabled pioneering individuals to construct within them highly personalized environments in opposition to more traditional living spaces: in this case, a monumental area of 1,670 square metres/18,000 square feet – combining areas for living and working ('I am outrageously anxious to live with my own work', Nesbitt said).[1] While Nesbitt's loft retained its integrity as part of a bohemian, artists' space, its emphatic luxury – of scale and texture – made it a clear departure from the earlier, uncompromisingly basic lofts inhabited by the likes of Rauschenberg and Lichtenstein.

The main architectural statement evident here was to slice through the centre of the loft, creating a 58 metre-square (625 foot-square) atrium roofed by an enormous skylight of aluminium and glass. Otherwise, the building was reduced to its barest essentials: original plank-wood floors, brick walls and cast-iron columns. In the words of the architect: 'I wanted to maintain the integrity of those parts of the building that were old, and at the same time clearly define the new.'[2] Knowles divided the loft into zones that focused around Nesbitt's daily schedule. The first floor was planned around the fibreglass swimming pool, which was, according to the architect, the largest indoor pool in any residential space in America at that time.[3] Nesbitt's bedroom and kitchen are also on this floor. The second level was designed as an entertainment space and a gallery, intended for both Nesbitt's own works, and as display space for other artists as well.

Terracotta tiles surrounding the pool led into the adjacent living areas (only the bathrooms had doors), presenting a mass of white leather furniture, tropical plants and assorted oriental *objets d'art*. The various floors were divided by 2.4-metre- (8-foot-) high partitions used to display the artist's work, while the living areas were defined by semi-open hexagonal spaces created by the partitions, and by groupings of plants and painted circles on the wooden flooring.

NOTES

1 _ 'Background for an Artist: Lowell Nesbitt's Studio: A Stable Remodeled', *Architectural Digest*, April 1977, p. 101.

2 _ *Ibid.*

3 _ *Ibid.*

2 The first-floor sitting room. The architect maintained the integrity of the interior of the building by isolating the bedrooms, bathrooms and kitchen within the core of the space, leaving the external walls free for the artist to display his large paintings. Plasterboard partitions define the area. In the words of *Architectural Digest*, the loft was 'an act of industrial archaeology in a city that has only begun to appreciate its past'.

3 Nesbitt's rooftop terrace.

4 The first-floor fibreglass pool, located below the atrium.

5 The centre of the loft, with its 58 metre-square (625 foot-square) atrium, carved through the centre of the three floors, and topped with an enormous skylight of aluminium and glass; a way of bringing light into a building that had windows only on its front elevation. Rampant ferns and semi-tropical plants peek out from the tiers of balconies, as well as the artist's painting of giant irises, from 1973.

5

2

4

3

1

1 Typical loft buildings in Kreuzberg occupy the back yard areas behind shops and houses. In the 1970s, loft dwellers occupied a series of these former factories as a political protest against their demolition. This block is in Currystrasse.

2 **3** Postcards from the 1970s by the artist and loft dweller Dieter Kramer, designed to warn against the effects of clearing old buildings in favour of new concepts in city planning.

In the late-1970s, artist and photographer Dieter Kramer documented a group of loft pioneers and campaigners who formed a community in a series of late-nineteenth-century buildings in the Kreuzberg district of Berlin. The result is an extraordinary visual record of life in the bohemian loft.

'It was the epoch of destroying all old buildings', recalls Kramer, who still lives in a converted factory in the district. 'The arguments of Le Corbusier for new city plans with big roads were still effective. It was only my generation that discovered the qualities of these old buildings. We wrote about them and published them and saved them in this way.' Kramer himself produced a series of campaign postcards that drew attention to the need to retain the buildings, which would otherwise have been demolished in the name of urban renewal.

The former light-industrial buildings occupied by these pioneer loft dwellers were mostly built in the 1870s, after the Franco-Prussian War. France paid Germany five billion gold francs in reparations and much of this money found its way into the urban development of Berlin, the new capital of the united Germany. 'At this time, it was normal to have a workshop in every backyard', explains Kramer. 'Typically, they were for making clothes, pianos, typewriters and for printing.'

Kreuzberg, Berlin

Loft Community
Dieter Kramer and others

The Kreuzberg lofts of the 1970s were very different from the chic apartments that now fill the buildings. Often they were used as combined workshop and living spaces, with businesses ranging from printing to toy making. Other lofts were occupied by gay-only or women-only co-ops. Many people lived in their spaces illegally, and inevitably there were problems with owners and authorities. 'But the biggest problem', recalls Kramer, 'was the heating'. The vast, draughty spaces were freezing in the winter and various ingenious methods for heating them were explored. 'Most of the pioneers made a room within a room for the cold winters', recalls Kramer, explaining the strange shed-like constructions that appear in his pictures. One architecture student called Rainer, who is still a loft dweller in Kreuzberg, built a series of organically shaped 'meditation' and 'love' pods in his loft to create warmer, more intimate areas within the larger whole.

In order to solve such problems, the loft dwellers had breakfast meetings together each Sunday. Large numbers would gather to discuss campaigns and heating tactics. 'It was a mixture of two things that saved the buildings in the end', says Kramer. 'The city had no more money and there was our resistance.'

Big changes have taken place in the area since the fall of the Berlin Wall. Now at the centre of the unified city, Kreuzberg is expensive and fashionable. While some of the pioneers in these pictures still live in their lofts, other buildings have been carved up by developers to make commercial shell units – the first of their kind in Berlin. 'There are very few bohemian lofts left now', says Kramer, describing the exodus of 'interesting people' to the run-down quarters of the former East Berlin. He concludes, 'Artists always go to a quarter that is cheap and neglected, then the richer people follow.'

4 5 6 For pioneer loft dwellers, keeping warm was a major problem. One solution was to build giant 'meditation' and 'love' pods (shown here with the architect Rainer who built them). Others built simple structures like garden buildings within their spaces, as well as using large oil heaters, as shown in illustration 4.

7 Each Sunday, communities of Kreuzberg loft dwellers would meet for breakfast to discuss their campaigns for saving the buildings. Many of the residents still occupy their lofts today.

8 Dieter Kramer, instigator of the Kreuzberg loft movement.

9 Two members of a women's co-op.

10 A group of art students took an old press from a printer, which they used to print children's books.

7

8

9

10

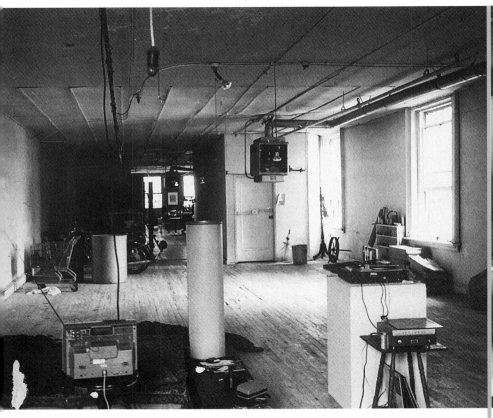

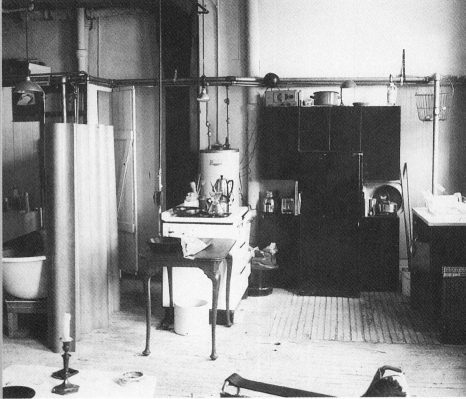

1

2

1 **2** Archive photos showing Henry Smith-Miller's Canal Street loft as it looked when he moved there in 1971. 'We furnished it with stuff from the street', he remembers. Nearly 30 years later, vestiges of this occupation remain in the space, which is now Smith-Miller's office.

Canal Street, New York

Smith-Miller Loft

Henry Smith-Miller

New York architect Henry Smith-Miller is now famous for the many notable lofts he has designed, but back in 1970, when he moved to the city, loft living was still considered to be part of an underground culture. 'There was a wonderful outlaw quality about living in these places', he remembers. 'SoHo was really run-down, the street lights didn't work and lots of the buildings were empty. There were only one or two bars.'

In 1971, Smith-Miller read an advert in the *New York Times* for a 780-square-metre (3,000-square-foot) loft apartment in a former typewriter factory in Canal Street. 'They wanted $1,000 key money', he recalls. 'When I got there, the most beautiful man I have ever seen in my life opened the door. Inside there was a gay commune of about 14 guys in black leather and chains who worked for Andy Warhol. Before them, Viva Superstar [a Warhol movie starlet] lived there. I paid the $1,000 and got the lease.'

Smith-Miller, who worked for the architect Richard Meier at the time, shared the open-plan 55-metre- (180-foot-) long apartment with a flatmate. 'First I had no privacy from my room-mate and then I got an Eames screen', he recalls. 'We furnished it with stuff from the street. I had a hideous blue sink that I found.' An early idea to suspend an Airstream caravan outside the building to house the services (this was the period of Archigram, remember) failed to materialize. Smith-Miller is frank about the conditions that loft dwellers lived in. 'There was no doorbell or phone. Brokers and bankers didn't want to live there. It was scary, but great.'

Later, when Smith-Miller began running his architectural studio from the loft, his staff would come up in the lift, which opens directly into the space. 'I had no way of getting in and out except past them', he says, 'so I had to get a second door.'

When Smith-Miller met his partner, Laurie Hawkinson, he moved into her loft around the corner and bought and retained his own loft as their architectural office. Vestiges of his time living there remain, including the kitchen units and the blue sink. However, other aspects of the loft have changed a great deal. 'Now it's one of my greatest assets', he says.

10th Arrondissement, Paris

Olla Loft

Els Staal, Interior Architect

'This loft has become a very liveable space, but it is in no means a finished and shining showroom of wealth', says Els Staal, the Dutch designer of this elegant but still gritty apartment, designed for Stefano Olla, a mathematician, in the rue du Faubourg Saint-Denis.

The 97-square-metre (1,044-square-foot) Olla loft, completed in 1997, is on the first floor of a six-storey factory building constructed around 1890. The building was originally used for clothing manufacture, as is still the case for the ground and third floors, and for around 60 per cent of buildings in the neighbourhood. The first four floors were formerly intended for industrial use with two floors of apartments above. Staal's approach to converting the space for domestic use has been to retain as much of the original form, industrial looks and open-plan quality of the space as possible. Many of the furnishings and fittings are re-used 'found' objects, such as the kitchen sink, the existing waxed oak floorboards and the industrial ironing and sewing tables. Other specially designed or adapted furniture is mounted on castors for easy reconfigurations of the space. Electricity is carried in surface-mounted galvanized-steel conduits. To maintain the open-plan vistas, the bathroom is enclosed by a wall that reaches only half way up to the height of the 3.5-metre- (11-foot-) high ceiling.

Lofts are still a rare phenomenon in Paris. According to Staal, the city is still conservative, with most people opting to live in compact spaces: Parisians, she says, are 'shocked' to see the size of this loft, although the idea is slowly gaining popularity.

Staal has shown what can be done with the city's run-down industrial buildings, at minimum cost. 'There was no budget for fancy finishes and furniture', she says of the FF230,000 budget. Instead, the result is what she calls 'an unconventional ensemble', which might frighten the *haute bourgeoisie*, but which would seem just like home to any loft dweller in SoHo, Kreuzberg or Shoreditch.

1

2 The kitchen area. Many of the furnishings and fittings in the loft are re-used found objects, such as the kitchen sink, the waxed oak floorboards and the industrial ironing and sewing tables (the ironing table is shown here). The curtains in the kitchen are made from frosted PVC, which filters out 60 per cent of the sun, while allowing light to pass through. The circular table is designed by the architect.

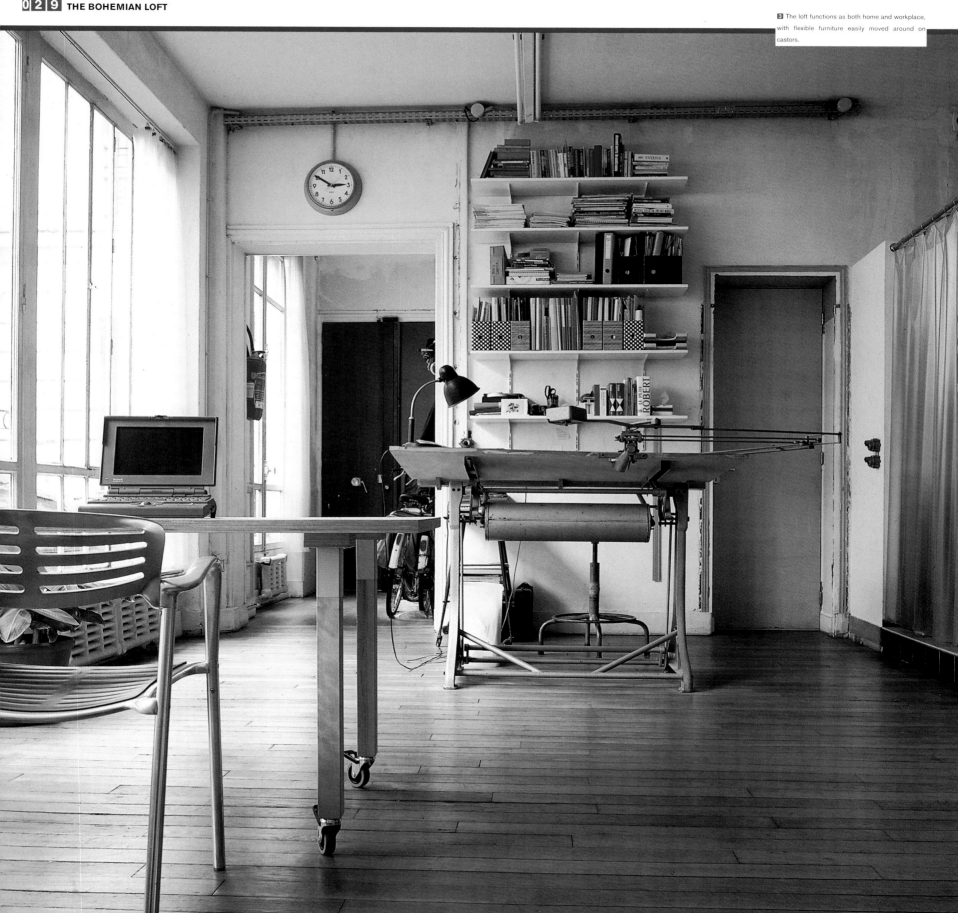

3 The loft functions as both home and workplace, with flexible furniture easily moved around on castors.

Neukölln, Berlin

Loft Commune

Sliwinski Hesse
Architects

Architecture often serves as a suitable metaphor for social and political concerns, and in the case of this loft in Neukölln, close to the centre of Berlin, this is particularly evident. Located on the third floor of a four-storey former turn-of-the-century laundry building and situated behind a rank of residential properties, the 240-square-metre (2,583-square-foot) loft resulted from the desire of two enthusiastic students – Sigi Sliwinski and Joachim Hesse – to experiment with a living space on a very limited budget.

Eschewing the familiar option of squatting, they decided to choose a legally secure option and negotiated a five-year lease with their landlord, which was later extended for a further five years. The idea was to create a commune of seven people within this loft, but this dwindled to four after a few months. They produced the idiosyncratic internal structure between 1983–85, using recycled materials obtained from the street to create seven separate sleeping areas, some contained by glazed wall units arranged in a haphazard pattern, others left more exposed to the general access areas of the loft. These different zones would be used on a rotational basis according to the varying needs – sexual or social – of the loft dwellers. The commune atmosphere extended to the toilet facilities – two were placed next to each other, with no barrier between them – while the bath was set on top of a raised platform that lay open to view from the rest of the loft. 'We really loved creating a freedom for ourselves in this space', says Hesse, 'but we found our parents didn't, when they came to visit.' As a reaction to the red tape and geographical divisions that went to make up so much of Berlin life – 'Berlin at that time really was a prison. The Wall hadn't yet come down, and the city was trapped by a hostile regime' – the students painted their own geometrical grids in red paint across the white concrete loft floor, forming elegant but pointed references to the arcane political pettiness defining the outside world.

The self-build process took two years; the first year to do the hard labour of breaking down existing partitions and firming up the existing structure (remember, they had to study during this period); the second year to complete the detailed work. The total cost amounted to DM15,000, which was divided equally by seven. At first, this bohemian lifestyle operated quite successfully, but, Hesse admits, it broke down when people started developing alternative relationships outside the domain of the loft. When new members came in, they would pay a suitable fraction of the on-going costs of the project. When the commune finally fell apart – the students left to pursue careers, or returned to their parents' homes – the loft was subdivided into glass cabins and lost its open sense of space and bohemian individuality. But Hesse made this experience the subject of his own university architectural thesis, so its lessons have not been entirely forgotton.

1 The eccentric bathing arrangements in this loft are made possible by a relaxed attitude to domestic conventions and a delight in salvaging from skips.

2

3

2 Removing unnecessary internal walls is a prerequisite for the ambitious loft dweller. Here, the Berlin students have started on the plasterwork stud walls, revealing in the process the elegant line of the loft beams above.

3 The main living area and kitchen reveals a loftiness, despite low ceilings, which in turn provide a villagey feel. A sleeping zone is at the far end of the space.

4 Plan of the 240-square-metre/2,583-square-foot communal residence.

5 Exterior of the former turn-of-the-century laundry building.

4

5

Garment District, New York

Miller-Jones Studio

LOT/EK Architecture

1 **2** The wall of the large container unit has been cut into to form three hinged doorways that lead into the sleeping area. When closed, these doors melt into the long aluminium wall that bisects the loft space; the fridge, television and video, cooker and sink unit thus appear as autonomous objects, frozen in a metal sea.

1

Located in the garment district of midtown Manhattan, the Miller-Jones studio is both a home and work space for Stephen Miller, a fashion photographer, and Christine Jones, a set designer. Situated on the 14th and 15th floors of a commercial building that still houses a clothes manufacturing business, the 204-square-metre (2,200-square-foot) space, completed in 1997, is divided along a diagonal axis into working and living zones.

LOT/EK Architecture's Ada Tolla and Giuseppe Lignano stripped the loft to its bare walls, a concrete floor and open ceiling cavities showing piping and ductwork. They painted the entire loft white, except for the bathroom, where they sealed the walls before lining them with waterproof acrylic panels. They then installed a partition wall that runs diagonally across the whole length of the loft. This defines the living and working spaces, and uses the 12-metre- (40-foot-) long side of an aluminium shipping container as the major organizational device. Tolla and Lignano cut into this impressive blade-like object to produce a series of hinged and pivoted panel openings that permit various degrees of physical and visual continuity with the rest of the loft space. Three of these panels rotate to open the bedroom, where Miller and Jones piled up metal filing cabinets and lockers to serve as built-in closets. Smaller panels in the aluminium wall reveal kitchen gadgets and facilities, as well as storage units for photographic equipment. Seen from the studio area of the loft, the aluminium wall is marked with strange graphic devices, reminders perhaps of the material's former existence within the holds of sea-going vessels. An imposing dining table on castors serves as another storage facility.

In using the aluminium container, Tolla and Lignano have followed a key principle of original loft living: to find something in the street and re-contextualize it in the loft, thus providing the object with a new purpose. The only difference is the scale of their ambition which, in this case, was justified by meticulous forward planning. The use of the container is also intriguing in that it acts as a metaphor writ large of the transitory, ever-mobile ethos of the early loft dwellers: eschewing the settled comforts of suburbia, these were individuals who were drawn to the restless, adventurous life of the larger horizon and the creative opportunities it offered. To live both inside and outside this container – it bisects the loft – is to suggest that its occupants could, if they wish, pack up and move on at a moment's notice, to hit the open sea in their container.

2

3 Hidden within the container unit, the kitchenette is practical and yet, when left exposed, presents a subtly crafted installation for visitors to the loft.

4 Plan showing how the 12-metre- (40-foot-) long aluminum shipping container diagonally bisects the Miller-Jones studio, both deconstructing and organizing the space. The 3.7-metre- (30-foot-) window runs the length of the space, providing a horizontal emphasis.

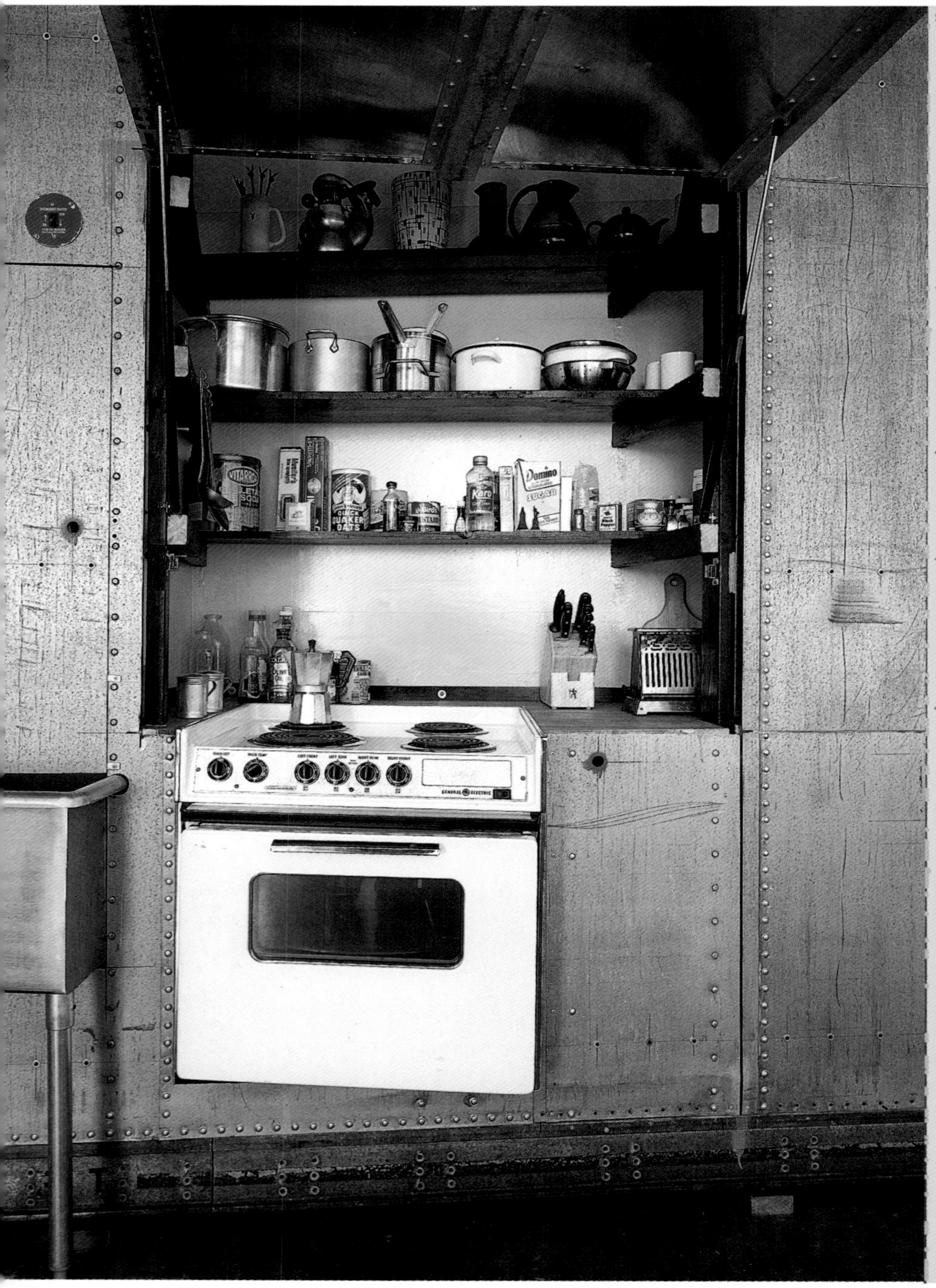

3

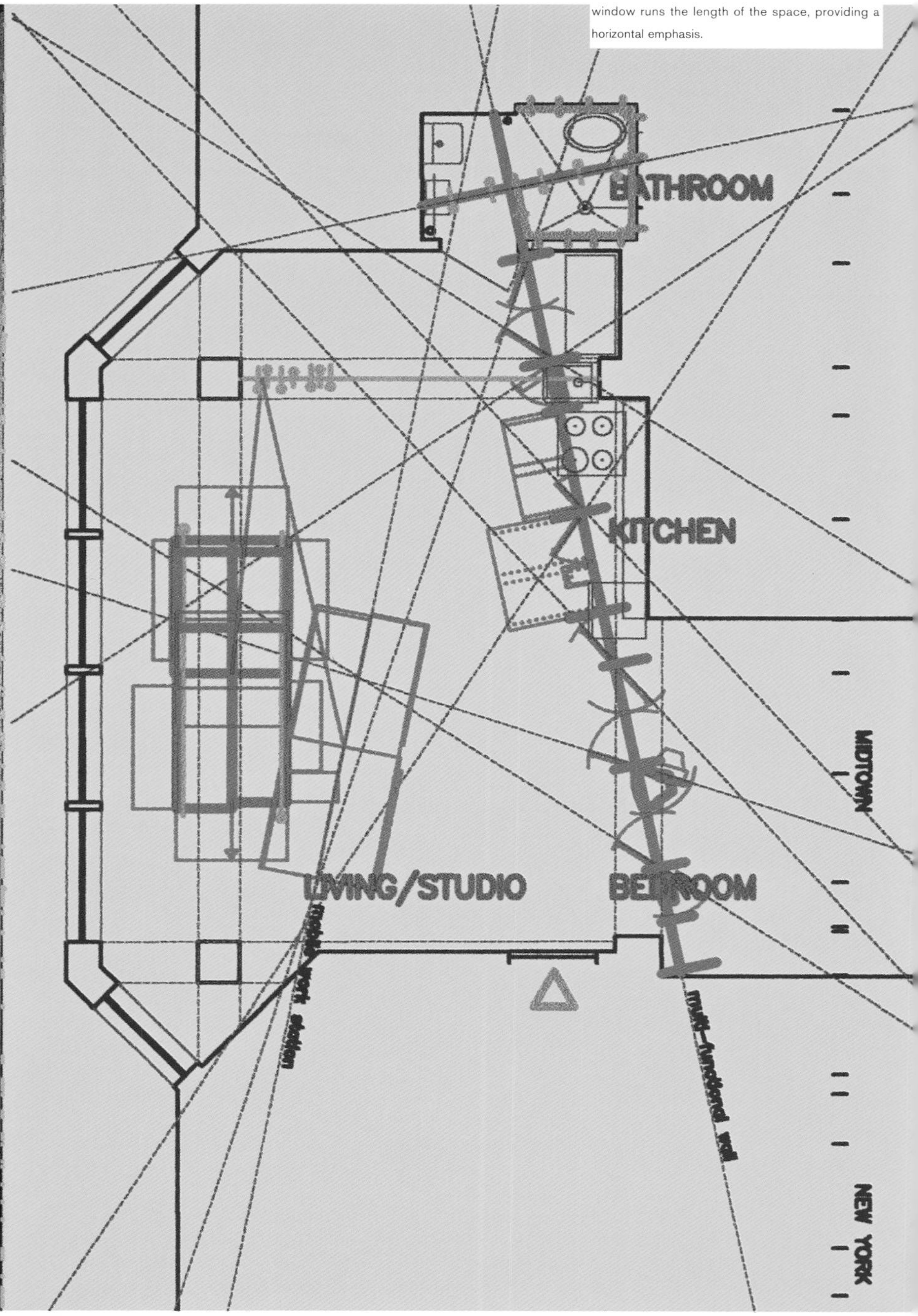
BATHROOM
KITCHEN
LIVING/STUDIO
BEDROOM
MIDTOWN
NEW YORK
multi-functional wall

4

5 The workstation area is set perpendicular to the aluminium container. The huge work table/dining table is made out of four disused fridges: doors open to provide extra storage.

6 The sealed-off private areas contribute to the
feeling of spatial openness.

7 Three full-height panels rotate to open the bedroom area. The Eames chairs were selected by the architects from Miller's collection of American furniture from the fifties, sixties and seventies. The filing cabinets and lockers continue the theme of metallic surfacing established by the aluminium wall panels.

Nostalgia: the loft and a romanticized past

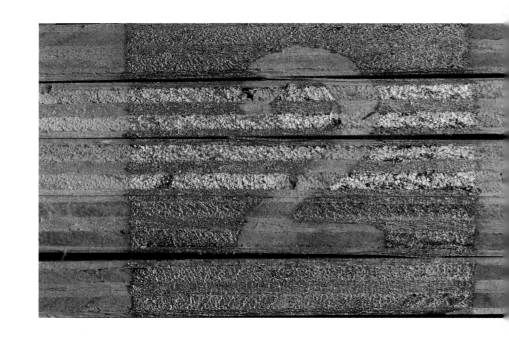

1 Early loft dwellers in New York were inspired by the quality of the buildings vacated by redundant industries. Among those who took an interest in the preservation of these buildings was the artist Donald Judd who bought a building in Spring Street in 1968 and restored it as a home and studio.

2 A warehouse building in London's Shoreditch, before conversion. Called The Factory, after Andy Warhol's space, the developers state in their brochure that the bare brickwork and other original fittings are to be cleaned and restored, in an attempt to keep alive the history of the place.

3 Overleaf: view of a disused cardboard manufacturers in London's Clerkenwell.

Only people who do not know the steam and sweat of a real factory can find industrial space romantic or interesting.[1]

The popular and now clichéd image of the loft, with its emasculated relics of pulleys and pipes and exposed brick walls and rows of columns, represents a heightened, climactic picture of a domestic building type, resulting from nearly 50 years of history. But the process by which this image has developed is surprisingly complex.

As we fall deeper into the post-industrial age, we view the industrial buildings of the past – formerly associated with sweat and misery – with a romantic eye. 'The mere fact of preservation aesthetizes, turning warehouse walls into townscape, derricks and cranes into obelisks, alleys into picturesque lanes', writes the historian Raphael Samuel. 'It makes back-wardness visually appealing and turns subjects of study into objects of desire.'[2] But when the first generation of loft dwellers occupied the crumbling industrial buildings of downtown Manhattan in the fifties, sixties and early seventies, the historic features and post-industrial detritus of these structures was by no means the unanimous draw.

'I do not believe in nostalgia', says Henry Smith-Miller, who as a young architect working for Richard Meier moved into his first New York loft in 1972. 'We couldn't afford nostalgia. The reasons were tectonic and economic. The only thing that was luxurious about a loft then was space. If there was stuff there, you just left it. I had a printing press that was too heavy to throw out. But I didn't want it.'

Smith-Miller, who worked as an architect on many early lofts in New York (including one for a

well-known artist in the mid-seventies, which he designed in return for a packet of cigarettes and a bottle of whisky), gives other practical reasons why 'the loft look' developed in a way that apparently celebrated the building's original structure and fittings. 'You really couldn't touch the walls in these buildings because they were so rotten. So what we did was colonize them. We made insertions. Loft living is a very nomadic idea.' Now living in a 'rental' loft in SoHo, Smith-Miller says he and his architect-partner Laurie Hawkinson have designed everything in their home to be removable.

For other pioneers in New York, however, the attitude was different. A new interest in the value and preservation of industrial buildings was born out of the post-industrial decline in manufacturing and the resulting 'rotten tooth', as Smith-Miller describes it, in the heart of the city. In

response to European models of post-war reconstruction, where whole swathes of cities were swept away and replaced with high-rise blocks and pedestrianized streets, urban theorists began to reconsider the aesthetic and regenerative value of existing infrastructure.

In her seminal and highly influential book *The Death and Life of Great American Cities*, first published in 1961, Jane Jacobs celebrates the rich diversity in cities that comes from old and new buildings standing alongside each other and the many forms of occupation they support. 'Among the most admirable and enjoyable sights to be found along the sidewalks of big cities', she writes, 'are the ingenious adaptations of old quarters to new uses.' Jacobs' argument was based on economic and sociological factors. 'In successful districts', she concluded, 'old buildings "filter up". Meanwhile, she added: 'Newness, and its superficial gloss of well-being, is

a very perishable commodity.' Loft dwellers must have been foremost in her mind when she said: 'Many city occupants and enterprises have no need for new construction.'[3]

But in addition to the pragmatic concerns of Smith-Miller and the economic and sociological arguments espoused by Jacobs, there was also a factor of romantic association at play even among early loft dwellers. As Sharon Zukin writes: 'A sense that the great industrial age has ended creates melancholy over the machines and the factories of the past.'[4] Campaigns to save buildings threatened with demolition were launched by artists and conservationists and some loft buildings were lovingly restored.

Among those who took an interest in the preservation of Manhattan's industrial heritage was the artist Donald Judd. In November 1968 he bought 101 Spring Street – a five-storey cast-iron framed building, originally constructed in 1870 – with the idea of restoring it as a space for

living, working and showing art. 'I thought the building should be repaired and basically not changed', he later wrote. Accordingly, the building was lovingly restored, with three floors given over to sleeping, eating and working respectively; the remainder was used as gallery space. 'The given circumstances were very simple', he wrote of this process. 'The floors must be open; the right angle of windows on each floor must not be interrupted; and any changes must be compatible.'[5] Judd's approach to retaining, restoring and celebrating the structure and form of his building, as well as his minimal arrangements within, and the subsequent buildings he restored in Marfa, Texas, has been adopted by many international loft dwellers, architects and developers in the decades that have followed.

Among the more recent generation of loft dwellers is the London-based architect James Soane. 'The whole question of what is authentic is a late-twentieth-century concern', he says on

the issue of whether original loft details should be retained as signifiers of the building's former use. 'The loft is not just an empty vessel. It has its own history written on it and you want to reveal that history.'

Soane has designed and lived in two London lofts with his architect partner, and in both they have adopted an approach that respects the existing building but that doesn't over romanticize its original features (as Soane points out, there's no longer any 'truth' attached to these relics anyway). 'The materials in a loft shell are to do with construction', he argues. 'The buildings were built as factories so they never bothered with finishes. There's no dressing up with another layer.' The approach of architects like Soane is to leave this 'raw' space in order to make a clear distinction between any new insertions. 'For us, this is always to do with juxta-position, to do with "occupation" of space', he says. The result is a contrast between the

transient, plasterboard construction, with its contemporary furniture and fittings, and the historic shell.

Back in New York, Diane Lewis, professor of architecture at Cooper Union and a practising architect, has been developing an approach to designing lofts since she first encountered them as a student in 1968. Lewis says that she was moved by the archaeological remains of Rome, where she spent some time living, and this gave her a 'consideration for the existential quality of the shell'. The architectural challenge of lofts, she says, is to 'develop a dialectic between what's new and the palimpsest of the shell.'

Lewis claims that her architectural ambition and vision of the perfect home is not clouded by an idealized view of the past. Rather, she sees loft architecture in the lineage of the Modern Movement programme. Quoting the modernist principles of free-plan space, and in particular

4 5 An established and respected architectural approach to the loft (here, an apartment of 1997 in London by architects McDowell + Benedetti) is to make contemporary insertions which are in clear contrast to the original materials and structure.

6 The original structure and industrial detailing of this building, formerly the North Dallas Power & Light Substation, has been celebrated and fetishized by its architects Gary Cunningham and Sharon Odum, in 1988.

7 The second loft of the architect Leslie Gill in Greene Street, New York, showing the way that a domestic environment can be built around the historical remnants of an unrelated past.

4   **5**

6   **7**

the domestic schemes of Mies van der Rohe, she says that the loft as a domestic form in many ways fulfils the principles of 'long-span' architecture, where 'the objects of existence – the sleeping room, the bathroom, the kitchen – become *meubles* or objects.' Lewis explains:
'My own desire to live in a complete space was more obtainable in the nineteenth-century shell than anywhere else in the city. It is ironic that the aspirations of the most advanced society have been realized in the ruins of the previous century.'

Having said this, Lewis is fascinated and deeply impressed by the technological advances made by the designers of the buildings that now act as hosts to many lofts. 'The ambition of those engineers was to get the structural system to carry all the necessary functions', she says. 'Inherent in all this cast-iron work is the beginning of the Modern Movement.' But, like many loft lovers, in celebrating the achievement of a past generation, Lewis also idealizes it. Her language reveals her passion as she describes the 'lacy delicacy' of the iron frames, or the view along the façades of 23rd Street that, she says, look Venetian. 'If you close your eyes', she implores, 'you can just imagine a canal there'.

For the large groups of student artists and political activists who occupied a series of former industrial buildings in the Kreuzberg district of Berlin in the mid-seventies, the concerns were rather different. 'It was about space, money and survival', says Dieter Kramer, an artist and

photographer who was one of the residents at that time. 'Artists always go to a quarter that is cheap and neglected, then the richer people follow.' There was no romanticising about the industrial detritus left in the lofts. 'They were full of old machinery', remembers Kramer. 'These things may be chic today, but then they were just thrown away.'

Clearly, there has been a shift between the need and desire for space described by early loft dwellers and the academic or fetishistic desire for signifiers of authenticity desired by the purchasers of the contemporary loft developments on both sides of the Atlantic. As Harry Handelsman, developer and chairman of Manhattan Loft Corporation, says of his first project in London's Summers Street in 1992, 'the concrete ceilings in the buildings were left unpainted so that [the development] would maintain its authenticity.' Photographed and presented seductively in the sales brochure, the original features of the industrial loft have become fetishized for the consumer. 'We were marketing a lifestyle', says Handelsman of his earliest brochure. 'And I'm very happy to do that.'

For Renato Benedetti, an architect in London who has worked on designs for a number of lofts, including his own, the approach to the shell and the industrial relics in a loft depends on their quality. 'Very often what remains can be very superficial', he explains. 'A cleaned up and disused pulley becomes fetishistic. When it appears on the cover of a brochure to generate an

idea about history when there was none, that's awful. Little things become marginal and lose their sense of reality. But the actual shell can be good and very "real" if you retain it and add new things that are distinct.'

Benedetti and his partner Jonathan McDowell carefully preserved and restored an original timber roof structure in a Grade I-listed warehouse loft in London's Docklands, and inserted juxtaposing modern services and devices to partition the space. 'As long as you're clear about what's being conserved and why, then I don't think you should feel uncomfortable', he concludes.

The romantic associations of the loft building are now manifold as the early loft dwellers' idealization of the industrial past becomes layered with a new generation's idealization of the bohemian lifestyle of the sixties and seventies. As Henry Smith-Miller points out, rich people who come on the scene later, when an area is fashionable, want to live like artists or 'how they think artists live'.

The current heightened obsession with the industrial details of loft buildings as they become more polished and more rarified is the cumulative effect of nearly half a century of loft living. For many people buying into the loft lifestyle, these details are the signifiers of having acquired that ideal. In our new age of digital technology and rapid change, our romance with an idealized

past has grown stronger. As the historian Robert Harbison has written: 'There is no nostalgia like the nostalgia for simpler machines, which are now imbued with the warm glow of a smaller past.'[6] It is this mythologized, slower and more simple life that many continue to seek out and celebrate through lofts.

NOTES

1 _ Sharon Zukin, *Loft Living: Culture and Capital in Urban Change* (Rutgers University Press, 1989) p. 59.

2 _ Raphael Samuel, *Theatres of Memory* (Verso, 1996) p. 304.

3 _ Jane Jacobs, *The Death and Life of Great American Cities* (Penguin, 1994) p. 207.

4 _ Sharon Zukin, *op. cit.,* p. 59.

5 _ Donald Judd, *Donald Judd* (exhibition catalogue, Boymans-van Beuningen Museum, 1993) p. 109.

6 _ Robert Harbison, *Eccentric Spaces* (Secker & Warburg, 1977) p. 53.

'I've lived in lofts for at least 20 years', says architect Malcolm Holzman, principal of Hardy Holzman Pfeiffer Associates, who currently shares one of New York's wittiest and most spectacular lofts with his partner Andrea Landsman. The 370-square-metre (4,000-square-foot) space is on the top floor of a 12-storey building constructed in 1898, which pre-dates its famous Manhattan neighbours, the Flatiron and the MetLife buildings. The couple bought the loft in 1986, when they needed more space. 'But it had to be somewhere that hadn't been worked over', says Holzman. 'By then it was hard to find a commercial space that was suitable.'

Finally, they discovered this steel-framed building with its spectacular views over the city, and began converting the top floor for living. 'It had been abused for 100 years', recalls Holzman. 'But I liked the distressed appearance, which records its history.' This in mind, the architects left much of the concrete-covered structure, pipework and other services exposed in their original state, while the 'wildly abused' timber floor has been stained.

Into this raw space they then inserted a series of contrasting interventions. Three enclosures have been made of different materials to define their functions. The first, an enclosure of green-stained particleboard, houses a private workroom and spare bedroom; the second is a central box of corrugated fibreglass with roll-up doors, which functions as a 'garage' storage area; and the final box in white-painted wood houses the bathroom and services.

Probably the boldest move in the space is the cladding of two long walls in unfinished imitation stone sheeting. 'I own lots of things that hang on walls', says Holzman, an avid art collector, 'and because the walls had pilasters, I had to bring

1 A raw, untouched loft apartment in New York is now a rare commodity, but architect Malcolm Holzman and his partner Andrea Landsman were lucky enough to find this one in 1986.

Gramercy Park, New York

Holzman/
Landsman Loft

Malcolm Holzman

2 Among the main moves in this spectacular and witty interior are the cladding of two walls in galvanized metal sheeting designed to look like stone, as well as the creation of a 'garage' storage area in corrugated fibreglass. The original structure of the building remains exposed and celebrated on the ceiling and floor.

everything out to make it flush.' The galvanized metal sheeting he chose to use for the walls is a proprietary product normally sold for cladding trailers and outhouses. In these circumstances it would normally be painted stone-colour, but Holzman has left it unfinished. 'I thought it would be amusing to have real bricks next to phoney bricks', he explains. All around the loft, Holzman has displayed his collection of work by celebrated painters and sculptors alongside his collection of pop-culture artefacts – including souvenir plates that are lined up along one wall: 'they're trash', says Holzman, 'but some of them are quite old'. On the windowsills, small souvenir models of New York landmarks confront the real things on the skyline.

The vast main living space gives the Holzman/Landsman family much pleasure. 'If you're going to live in a loft, it's ridiculous to chop it up and make it into an apartment', says Holzman. 'Here, my son rides his in-line skates and we can have 100 people to dinner sitting at tables.'

3

4

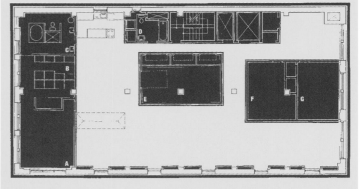

5

a _ bedroom
b _ dressing room
c _ bathroom
d _ bathroom
e _ storage
f _ workroom
g _ workroom

0   5

3   **4**   **6** In contrast to the cautious approach of many architects, Holzman has juxtaposed the original structure and details of his loft with collections of pop ephemera, art and colourful contemporary finishes.

5 Plan of the Holzman/Landsman loft.

6

1

In Italy – a country where history has left its architectural footprint everywhere, the renovation of lofts has been slower to catch on than in London or New York. There are simply too many classical, medieval or baroque ruins demanding attention, and it might be argued that industrial warehouse spaces come fairly low on the list of priorities as far as architectural preservation is concerned. Miki Astori, architect and furniture designer for the Italian company Driade, shares the space, completed in 1993, with Marina Verga. It is situated in central Milan, on the ground floor of what was originally a stabling block, then a carpenter's workshop, then assumed into a private house, and then converted back again into a light-manufacturing unit – a series of metamorphic transitions reminding one that in Italy, buildings have led many lives.

The 70-square-metre (753-square-foot) space displays many of the features one would expect to find in the stereotypical loft: brick walls, cast-iron columns, large glazed windows, high ceilings and an expanse of wood flooring. It looks on to a 30-square-metre (322-square-foot) courtyard, and nestles within a mixed residential/commercial sector of the city.

This loft is a rarity in Milan. 'You cannot find big spaces in the city to live in', says Astori. 'There simply isn't an existing tradition of living in

Milan, Italy

Astori/Verga Loft

Miki Astori

1 This loft contains the rustic appeal of a country cottage, evident in the exposed wooden beams of the ceiling and the brickwork arch, combined with the shop-designed aesthetic of the urban loft.

2 Miki Astori's loft in Milan, in which the designer lives and occasionally works. Elegant remnants of the building's industrial past include the slim cast-iron pillar and metal-framed windows.

3 The open-plan kitchen is both friendly and discreet, with single rattan blinds contrasting with the stainless-steel worktops and brick walls.

industrial warehouses, as loft living sits rather uncomfortably in the Italian mind. We live in traditional spaces – in Milan, most residential housing is of a bourgeois nature', he says. 'I designed some furniture from natural materials which matched those already in the building: the table is made from the same maple staves used in the floor, assembled on a rough ironwork frame. This is echoed by the materials used in the sleeping platform, which serves as a bed', Astori explains. The only interior partition to the loft is a sliding *shoji* in the Japanese style, made of a pinewood frame and a textile covering.

Significantly, it seems that, despite the initial appearance of a genuine loft – the rattan chaise longue by Driade, the Thonet bentwood chairs, the stainless-steel work surfaces in the Driade-designed kitchen, and the metalwork windows – there are some indicators (the brickwork arches, the classically inspired architrave to the doorway, the stone pillars and the vertical rails of the radiator echoing the ribs of a giant fluted column) of an architectural sensitivity, a respect even, towards the memory of arched viaducts, vaulted thermae and cavernous ruins.

1

2

Helsinki, Finland

Sopanen & Sarlin Loft

Marja Sopanen & Olli Sarlin

According to young architects Olli Sarlin and Marja Sopanen, strict residential planning regulations are the reason for the slow migration of the loft phenomenon to Finland. The situation is slowly changing, however: the authorities are beginning to encourage redevelopment in Helsinki's downtown area within former offices and light-industrial buildings.

Decades of accretions have carefully been removed from Sarlin and Sopanen's ground-floor loft apartment to reveal the robust details of a former textile factory. The red-brick building, in downtown Helsinki, was originally built in 1928. When the architects first visited the site, they found the space occupied by a cluster of partitioned offices. Suspended ceilings and multi-level floors had been added at various times over the building's 70-year history.

1 Loft culture has been slow to develop in Finland, where this former textile factory in Helsinki has recently been converted to loft apartments.

2 Young architects Olli Sarlin and Marja Sopanen have cleared out later accretions and restored the original open-plan form of the interior.

3 **4** The architects' design for the loft respects the original form and purpose of the building. New partitions (housing the bathroom) stop short of the ceiling. The second-hand kitchen units were originally designed for industrial use. The new pine floor in the L-shaped apartment is laid on joists made out of timbers reclaimed from other parts of the building.

3

4

5

The aim of the project, completed in 1997, was to uncover the original volume and structure of the factory and convert the space into a large 85-square-metre (914-square-foot) open-plan apartment. Partition walls were removed and the suspended ceilings stripped away. Underneath, the architects discovered shuttered-concrete beams. These were cleaned and sealed with a mixture of wallpaper paste and beer, as were the newly exposed red-brick walls (according to the architects, beer mixed with pigment is the traditional way to colour wooden walls). The timber joists from the ceiling were reused as studs for the floor and a new bleached and oiled pine floor laid on top. This floor stops just short of the wall to allow radiator pipes through without having to make messy holes.

The L-shaped apartment is arranged with the bathroom and kitchen situated at the shorter end of the plan and a 60-square-metre (645-square-foot) open-plan living and sleeping area running across the full width of the building.

The bathroom occupies a new plywood structure, which also forms the housing for the oven and kitchen cupboards. The bathroom enclosure stops short of the ceiling to indicate its newness and provide storage space above. Almost every other element in this apartment is mobile, including a piece of old hospital furniture that can be used to divide the sleeping area from the living room.

Recycled materials have been widely used in this project. Much of the plumbing is second-hand, as are some of the kitchen units, which were originally made for institutional use.

5 6 Every detail of the loft has been painstakingly restored as a celebration of the pre-war utilitarian building type. The bedroom partition is a piece of old hospital furniture.

7 Plan. The apartment runs the whole length of the building.

8 The ground floor of the former textile factory, before the start of renovation in 1996.

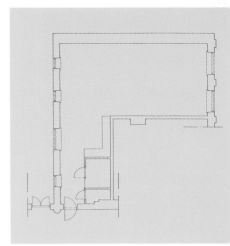

7

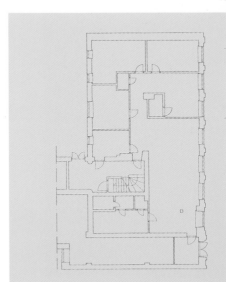

8

6

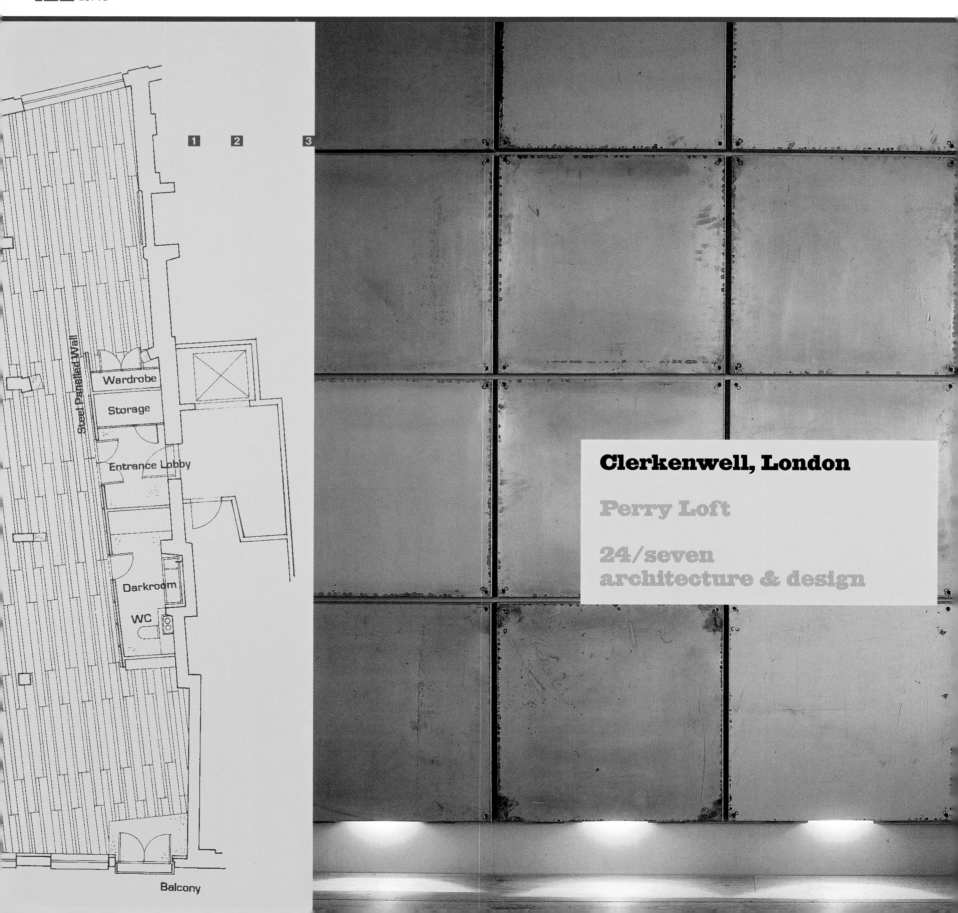

1 2 3

Steel Panelled Wall

Wardrobe

Storage

Entrance Lobby

Darkroom

WC

Balcony

Clerkenwell, London

Perry Loft

24/seven
architecture & design

In the property boom of the late 1990s the London loft has become a highly compromised commodity. Contemporary examples are often small shell units carved out of former industrial buildings by opportunist developers, which are sold to gullible clients at inflated prices and then over-designed by second-rate architects.

This loft in the Clerkenwell area of London, completed in 1998, is an exception. Designed by 24/seven architects Zoe Smith and Graeme Williamson for Mike Perry, the vast, rugged interior remains a celebration of 'industrialness' while drawing on original loft values to provide an open-plan space for uninhibited living.

What first attracted Perry to the apartment, part of a former factory built for Scholl footcare products in the 1920s, is its sound-proof concrete structure. 'I didn't want to worry about noise', he says. 'I can work late, then come in and play music really loudly and not bother anybody.'

Once he had settled on the 167-square-metre (1,797-square-foot) space, Perry gave his young architects a brief for an apartment which would remain open-plan and rugged. 'The beautiful thing about this place is the brick and concrete', he says. 'I wanted to keep as much of it as possible. I don't understand people who want to put rooms in lofts or over-design the interiors.'

For 24/seven, the challenge was partly about preventing the developer of the building from over finishing the space. 'We kept trying to stop the builders from painting the walls', recalls Smith. In the end, the walls were selectively stripped to reveal the most interesting, scarred parts of the brick and render stripped from the columns, which in turn exposed original glazed tiles.

Perry was keen that the space should be left raw enough to take his bohemian mishmash of old and new furniture. New finishes and fittings are therefore appropriately industrial and tough looking. A solid oak floor has been laid over the original concrete and the new block containing the entrance lobby, darkroom/lavatory and storage cupboards has been clad with reclaimed raised floor tiles. These are fixed with their textured and patinated steel undersides facing out, like a contemporary take on traditional panelling.

The other major interventions into this space are the kitchen units and the bathroom platform. The kitchen – which looks rugged enough to serve a canteen – is constructed in mild steel with a clear powder-coated finish and a polished-concrete worksurface. Next to it is the apartment's most impressive feature and claim to authentic loft status – an unenclosed bath, shower and basin raised up on a concrete plinth. 'I had always wanted to lie in a bath in a big open space', says Perry. 'And now I just wheel over the telly and watch it in the bath. It's magnificent.'

1 2 3 The entrance lobby of the Perry loft is ingeniously clad in reclaimed raised floor tiles reversed to expose their metal undersides.

4 5 The architects have roughed-up the standard developer's shell to regain some of the qualities of the early bohemian loft. Paint has been stripped from brickwork and tiles and appropriately rugged finishes and fittings installed. The floor is in oak, the custom-made kitchen in mild steel and the bathroom – open plan as in early lofts – is raised on a cast-concrete platform. The result represents a contemporary (and expensive) take on New York loft life in the late sixties.

6 7 8 Views, and plan, showing the huge open-plan bathing space and the sleeping area.

4   **5**

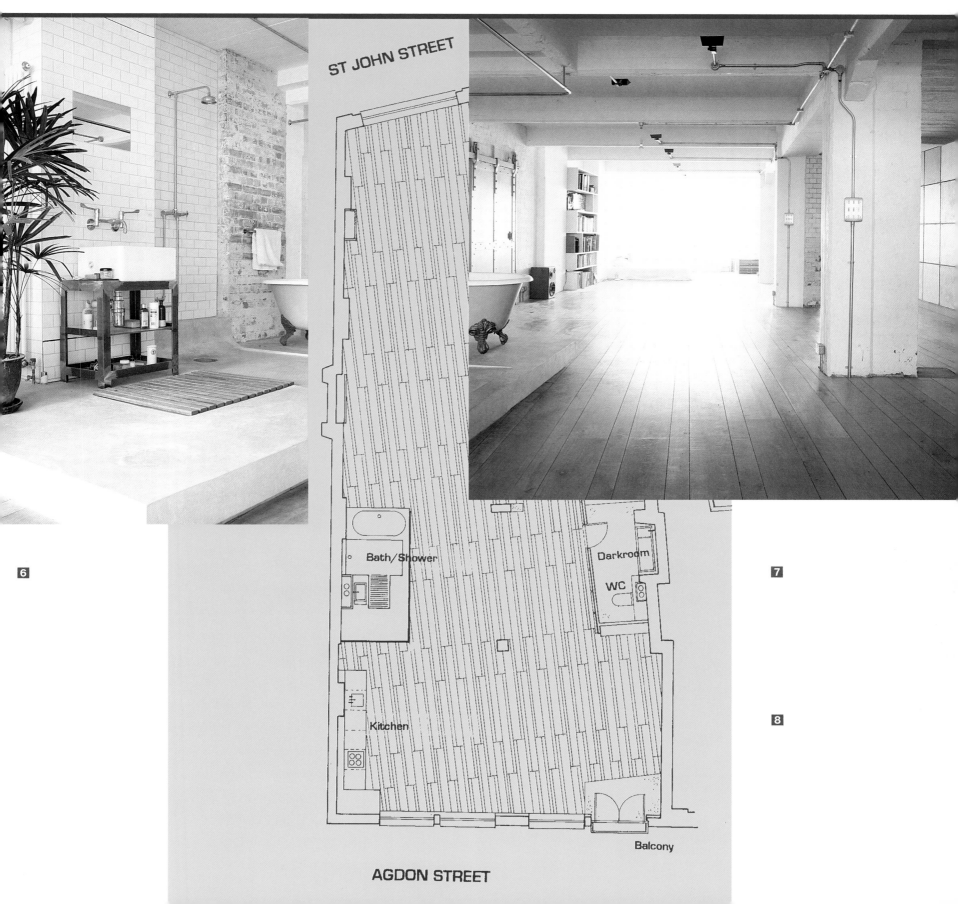

6

7

8

ST JOHN STREET

Bath/Shower

Darkroom

WC

Kitchen

Balcony

AGDON STREET

Washington Square, New York

'Urban Atelier' Loft

Diane Lewis Architect

1

Native New-Yorker Diane Lewis first experienced the loft district of Manhattan when she started architecture school at Cooper Union in 1968. 'In those days the streets were deserted', she recalls. 'It was like a Hopper painting.' Most of the loft dwellers at this time were artists and Lewis remembers Barnett Newman frequenting the local café and Ad Reinhardt living in a loft on Broadway.

Thirty years later, Lewis is professor of architecture at Cooper Union and a loft dweller herself, occupying a loft completed in 1993 in a small brick-and-timber building originally constructed in 1870 as a woodworker's shop in the historic Washington Square district of the city (woodwork for the surrounding churches was originally made here). 'It's extremely rustic', she says.

Lewis's approach to creating an office and library on the first floor and a home for herself on the second has been, she says, 'to develop a dialectic between what's new and the palimpsest of the shell'. Maintaining an open-plan space across the 10-metre (32-foot) depth of the building was important for the architect, who was determined to set the apartment within the lineage of the Modern Movement. To achieve this, partitioned spaces are, she says, treated as '*meuble*' within the volume. Her choice of iconic modern furniture by designers like Eileen Gray and Harry Bertoia reinforces the Modern Movement connection. 'The space is an abstract, platonic volume', she says, 'a space in which the elements of your life look expandable.'

In contrast to the highly detailed and slick finish of the new insertions, the original wooden joists and brick walls of this project have been left with their layers of old paint (what Lewis calls 'their chromatic changes') exposed 'to reflect occupancy'. In addition to the large amount of natural light that floods the space from both sides, artificial lighting has been

2

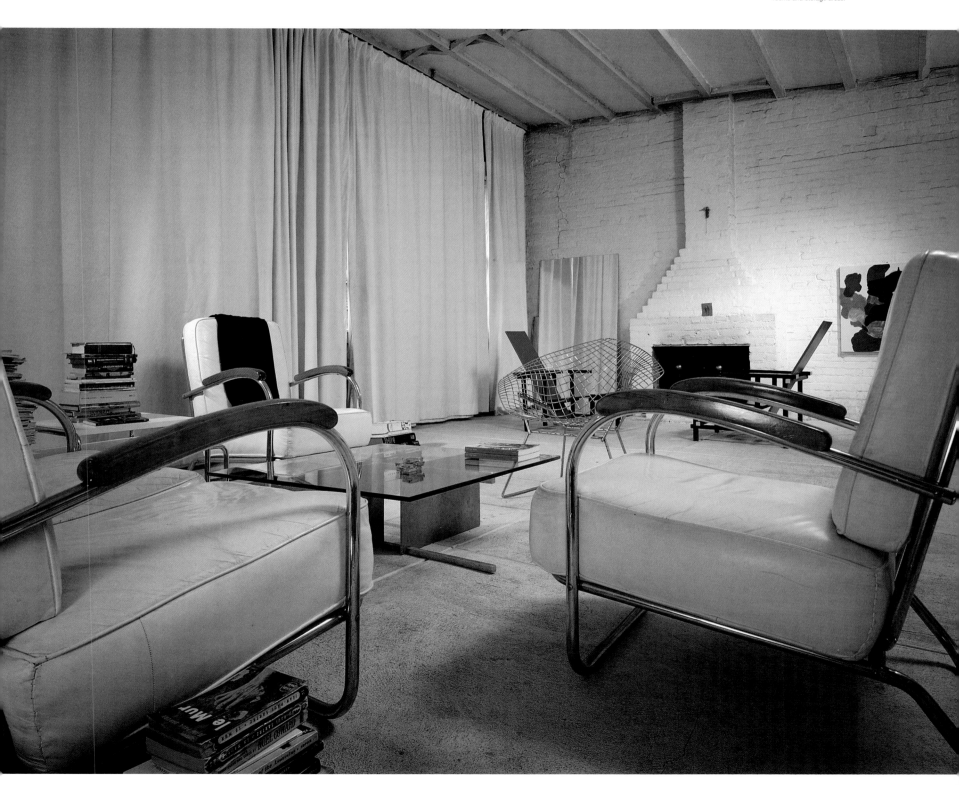

carefully inserted 'to illuminate and exaggerate the ruinous quality of the shell'.

'All the walls have programme', says Lewis of the newly inserted painted plywood partitions which shape the space. Some contain bookshelves, others drawers, cupboards and even an easel and lectern. The original gas radiators – an unusual and experimental heating system – have been reconnected and now provide warmth in winter. New floors in poured thin-set white concrete are made perfectly level, says Lewis, to contrast with the raw finish of the aged shell.

For Lewis, this project is a home and workplace, but as a scholar, she also approaches lofts as a serious academic issue. 'If you love the existing condition', she says, 'keeping that alive when you insert the new is the challenge architecturally.'

3 The plan shows how the private entrance from the street to the stairway arrives directly at the first-floor loft, containing Lewis's office, with a meeting area, drafting room, workshop and library. The stairs continue up to the second floor residence and library.

4 The study area, with its mix of Modern Movement furniture.

5 A partitioned space. Treated like furniture, the walls are each assigned a function.

4

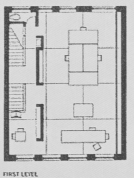

FIRST LEVEL   SECOND LEVEL

5

1

This floor of a former rag-trade factory had various incarnations as a transvestite nightclub and student flat before architects James Soane and Christopher Ash refitted it for their own home in 1994.

Because the space was rented, the architects wanted to spend a minimum amount of money. With a budget of £5,000, they installed storage heaters and refurbished the basic concrete, steel, timber and brick structure, leaving many of the original industrial relics exposed. A long studwork wall was inserted across the full width of the space to create two sleeping rooms and a bathroom. The bathroom fittings came from a salvage yard, the stainless-steel sink and catering unit were inherited in the space and the kitchen cupboards came from IKEA.

Alicia Pivaro, the director of the Architecture Centre at the Royal Institute of British Architects, and architect Paul Monaghan now live in the 130-square-metre (1,400-square-foot) loft. 'It's not necessarily an aesthetic that either of us would necessarily choose', says Monaghan of the apartment's raw looks, which recall those of early bohemian lofts. 'It's rough and ready, but because it's rented, any investment in it would have to be able to be taken out of the door.'

There are plus sides to the grittiness, though. 'We have huge parties', says Pivaro, 'and when we wake up in the morning, we just clear the bottles away and it looks fine again.' But like the real lofts of the early days, this space does not have new windows or insulated walls. 'So it's quite frighteningly cold in the winter', she says.

The loft's raw aesthetic also extends to the outside. Like the early lofts of Manhattan,

1 **2** Unlike the recent developer-led London lofts that are often small, expensive and super slick, this apartment harks back to a time when the attraction was about maximum space for minimum cost. With little alteration to the shell, the raw space provides a strong backdrop to the chaos, clutter and communal nature of modern life.

French Place, Shoreditch, London

Pivaro/Monaghan Loft

Project Orange

2

there are the remnants of old signs on the brickwork, handwritten new ones, and bits of cord and wire attached to the bells inside. The stairway is lined with padlocked doors and dirty brickwork, a far cry from the sanitized lobbies of developer lofts. 'It doesn't do any good to draw attention to it anyway', says Pivaro, referring to the burglars who prowl around smarter developments.

This loft is in the Shoreditch area of London, which has become highly fashionable since the couple moved in. 'The fact that it's become popular has become a real pain', says Monaghan, who is tired of the packed bars and littered streets. Still, the regeneration hasn't yet extended to an influx of shops. 'If you want to get a pint of milk, it's hideous', he says.

But both are happy with the flexible space loft living offers. 'It's about cooking a meal while the other person is sitting in the corner doing something completely different', says Monaghan. 'It has a chaotic charm', says Pivaro, adding that the mice with which they share the space are the only downside. 'It's not the nicest side of lofts', she says.

3

3 The stainless-steel sink and catering unit in the kitchen were original to the loft, and recall the building's previous life.

4 Large-scale entertaining is an integral part of loft culture (think Andy Warhol and Robert Rauschenberg). Here, Project Orange architects James Soane and Christopher Ash, far right, and current occupier Alicia Pivaro, far left, invite their friends to keep up the tradition.

4

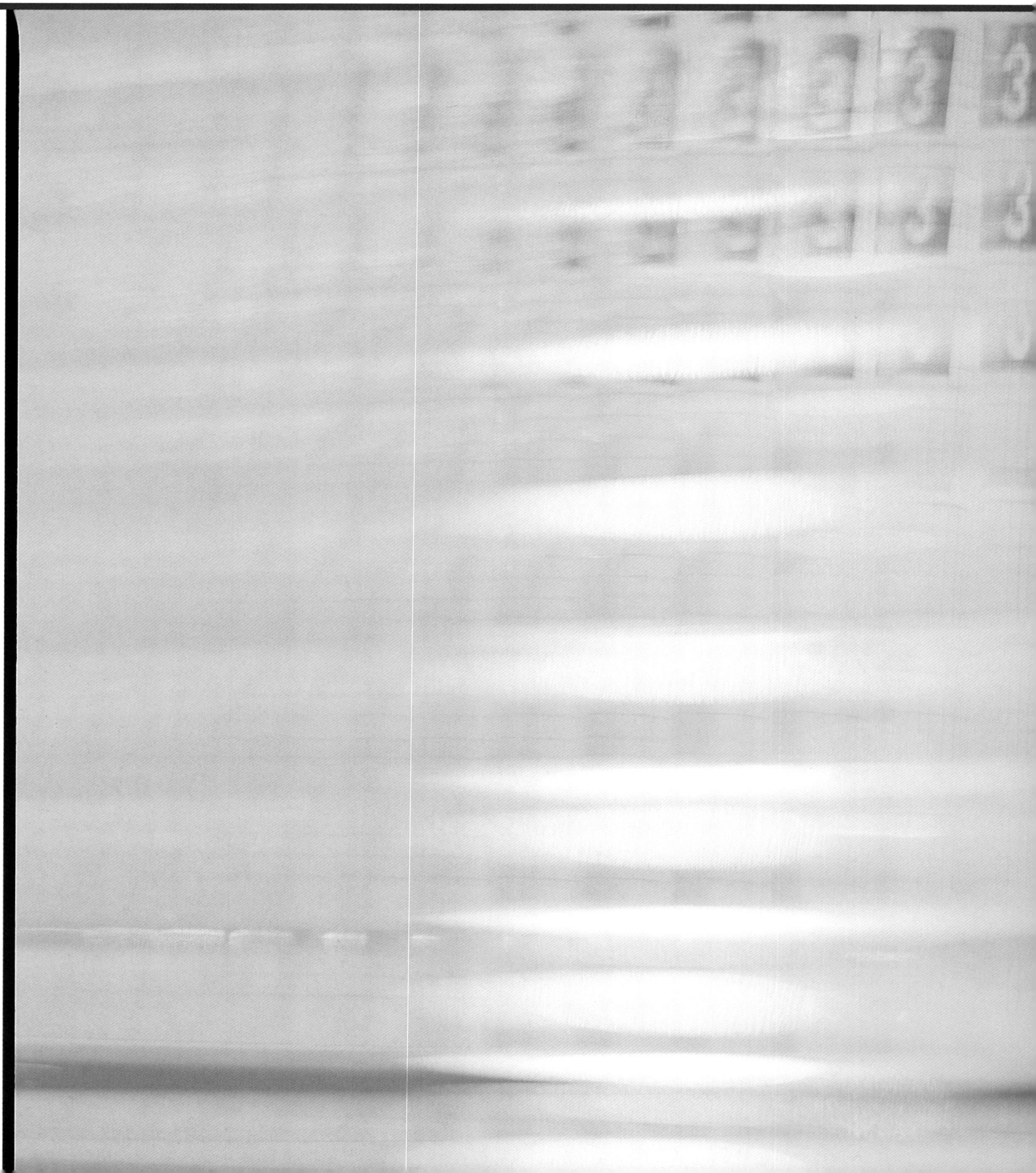

An urban sanctuary

1 John Constable, *The Hay Wain*, 1821, National Gallery, London.

2 L. S. Lowry, *Coming from the Mill*, 1930, Salford Art Gallery.

Living in a completely open loft allows me to be in charge of the space. Everything is an expression of my personality.[1]

These words – spoken by Martin Kippenberger about his loft in the Kreuzberg area of Berlin – underline the accuracy of Gaston Bachelard's observation in his seminal work *The Poetics of Space* that 'the house even more than the landscape is a psychic state'.[2]

Kippenberger's sentiments are commonplace to many loft dwellers, and remind us how much the realm of psychology permeates that of architecture. As a landscape of opportunity and a zone of liberation, the loft stands in stark contrast to many conventional living spaces, whether it be the brownstone, the purpose-built mansion block, the Victorian terraced house, or the suburban semi-detached home. Internally, the loft presents an absence of interior walls, predestined lay-out and conventional hierarchy of upstairs and downstairs. Externally, its relation to the street is also unique: the renovated loft offers an ambiguous public face and is therefore neither a working factory nor exactly a home. Indeed, this ambiguity is part of the *frisson* that has made loft living so appealing. There is no front lawn, garden gate, concierge'd foyer, or polite porch. The loft is a different space, one that proposes an escape from the standard conventions of domestic living.

In saying that the loft represents a form of urban sanctuary, one risks the charge of perversity. At first instance, the phrase itself seems oxymoronic when set against the enormous tradition in Western culture of the rural idyll, one illustrated by an age-old sequence of pastoral models, from the bucolic images of rural life conjured up in Virgil's *Georgics* to works of art produced by artists as diverse as Rubens, the most powerful advocate in paint of *vita ex urbe*, and 'The Hay Wain' by the nineteenth-century artist John Constable, whose alluring images of country

3 Negroponte loft in New York's SoHo, designed in 1974 by Henry Smith-Miller. The sparse, gallery-like interior is surely intended to be an internal, contemplative space.

3

scenes still stand in many people's eyes today as the ideal form of rural harmony. One only has to look at the paintings of grim city life produced by L. S. Lowry to believe that cities are what we flee from, and not towards. To speak of the possibility of the city serving as a place of refuge, a space for mental and physical recuperation thus seems absurd. How else do we explain the existence late in the twentieth century of heritage-obsessed aspirational magazines in the UK such as *Country Life* and *Country Living* and in the US, *Better Homes and Gardens*, *Southern Life* and *Town and Country*, with their pornographic attention to gracious estates, undulating landscapes and distressed furniture detail?

But if one considers how much the terraced house or the suburban home – with their conventional divisions of masculinity and femininity and their uneasy division between the formal and the informal, the public reception and the private moment – have been zones of

containment, oppression and inevitably, neurosis, then the notion of the loft as a sanctuary from these 'norms' is perhaps more accessible. Indeed, the domestic ideal 'remains throughout the course of modernism a crucial site of anxiety and subversion'.[3] This is not perhaps surprising, since domesticity per se has long been regarded as antagonistic to modernism, which has deliberately celebrated the energy, forms and attitudes of urban life. In 1923, Le Corbusier famously railed against the sentimental hysteria of the 'cult of the house', professing his determination instead to create 'a machine for living in', a statement that followed on from Adolf Loos' verdict that 'ornament' – supposedly that most bourgeois compulsion – was 'a crime'. Freed from the trappings of the bourgeois home, the aspirant loft dweller can thus embark on 'a heroic odyssey on the high seas of consciousness, with no time to spare for the mundane details of home life and housekeeping'.[4] As Sharon Zukin has observed, 'loft living is part of a

4 Mattes-O'Brien Loft, Lower Broadway, New York. Completed in 1996 by the architect Dennis Wedlick, the 278-square-metre (3,000-square-foot) space consists of two bedrooms, three bathrooms and large living areas. Shown here is the spectacular roof garden designed by Margie Ruddick. Set against a skyline that includes the twin towers of the World Trade Center, it confounds all notions of urbanity. The fact that it belongs to a loft is all the more extraordinary.

larger modern quest for authenticity', a view with which the architect Diane Lewis – long-time resident in New York – concurs.[5] For Lewis, while the suburban family structure has been revealed as potentially abnormal, the loft is 'a genuine piece of urbanity. It's about being in the inner city. Biting the bullet, so to speak. It's a kind of a removal, being in the dead centre of things'. She considers that the spatiality of the loft represents a sanctuary in itself, and that this palatial spaciousness enables the loft dweller to free his or her possessions and furnishings from the burden of being merely decorative: 'The first loft dwellers were existential in the way they arranged their possessions. By accepting the existing conditions of the loft environment – the brick walls, the large floor space, the columns – and placing their possessions within it, they found that there was no distinction between art and life, between the real and the ephemeral. The suburban aesthetic is seen as supercilious, whereas in the urban space you face the fragility of your life against the fabric of the city.' This experience has, Lewis says, kept her feeling spiritually alive.

Lofts, therefore, present an architectural equivalent of the social space that the postmodern intellectual occupies in Western society: linked to the city, but not satisfactorily framed by suburban values, instead finding value in the archaeology of centres of production while not being subject to their economy. It is, above all, individual. This blurring of art and life, of living, as it were, on the knife-edge of urbanity, relates to a broader perception of loft living as something intimately linked to the existential experience of art-making itself. Zukin has underlined the importance of 'the sense of adventure of the artists' ambience which still clings to living in a loft neighbourhood'.[6] With their dynamic, dangerous lives – at least, from the suburbanites' point of view – artists lent a precious allure to loft spaces, associating them with notions of originality, daring and rebelliousness. And it was an existential act to transplant yourself in a piece of the rough city (bearing in mind that in the early days, living in lofts in Manhattan, the heartland of loft living, was illegal until 1976). These lofts were therefore, by location and legal necessity, difficult to find, tracked only through maze-like, unlit passages, removed from the density of bustling streets, their anonymity held behind metal doors with broken doorbells, all serving to mythologize a journey of discovery. But then this only adds to the value of the goal.

And the result of this journey? The recognition that, after all, the city, its silhouettes, textures and sounds, were desirable in themselves. 'I wanted to experience the city at every level – to feel the view and the light. The idea was to be connected to the city and the sky.... The trick was to eliminate distraction.' So enthuses architect Lee Mindel in an issue of *House & Garden* entitled 'Modern magic – the ultimate in loft living'.[7] His words could be those of any loft dweller. 'It's the ultimate observation spot', he continues. 'The space has an interior panorama. The idea is to make it dynamic, like the city; to keep the volume open, so you see the city no matter where you are'. And in that internal panorama, the single most important feature is the loft dweller himself. For not only is the space designed to allow seigneurial command of the city: its vast, cavernous dimensions are there to accommodate his or her own sense of themselves, where people like Kippenberger can say, in all modesty, that 'everything is an expression of my personality'. Lofts, therefore, are spaces of possible identities, spaces in which the dream of what you want to be can be lived out, just as those loft pioneers working the Klondike of real estate – the action painters of 1950s Manhattan – had done: 'it was in the studio that the artist constantly recreated his self'.[8] Note the masculine emphasis. For the loft represents a brave territory compared to the feminization of the traditionally domestic home.[9]

5 View of a north-London penthouse loft designed by Stanton Williams in 1997. The apartment was featured in a British television documentary for Channel 4 on the subject of minimalism. In the programme, the owner expressed her concern that the colour of the sycamore floor might in fact be too distracting – and therefore not sufficiently minimal.

The openness of the loft environment – 'so you see the city no matter where you are' – and its (supposed) absence of standard domestic hierarchies – presents a reassuring, 'honest' visibility, one that, to apply the phrase the artist/photographer Jeff Wall used to describe the glass offices of Mies van der Rohe, is open to the witness of the rational and alert citizen and is therefore 'without the cabals and conspiracies characteristic of aristocratic and religious obscurantism'.[10] Glass walls are features commonly found in lofts, both on the external façades and used internally to delineate separate living zones while maintaining a sense of transparency. But, as Wall observes, 'this openness brings its own oppression, in that nothing can be kept secret or hidden' – an irony not lost on any architect charged with the design task of maintaining the spatial integrity of the loft while allowing for privacy in areas such as bathrooms.[11] Openness also has implications on the acoustic values in a loft. When asked about their experience of living in their Nile Street loft in London's Shoreditch area, architects Steven Bowkett and Jane Tankard, who have a small daughter, ruefully admit that there is little opportunity for privacy in the expanse of their loft: 'it means you can get on top of one another rather a lot', Bowkett says, with classic British understatement.

This dilemma, of course, merely highlights, albeit tangentially, the frustrating tyranny of Mies' basic design principles – 'almost nothing' and 'less is more'. Excessive openness, according to Wall, is 'the reflex of an extreme inwardness... leading to the fetishizing of the self's personality within an anonymous and "perfect" system'.[12] Withdrawal and relaxation, in the presence of such all-round surveillance, 'becomes tense and compulsive'.[13] And it is when people such as Lee Mindel, a loft dweller and designer, refer to the loft as 'almost like a curated space, because each of the objects has an integrity and a discipline that the place has', where these objects 'have a dialogue with each other', that we understand the easy transition the loft makes from being an urban sanctuary to being a sanctified space, one akin to the hushed environs of the contemporary art gallery.[14] When you consider the ecclesiastical nature of many sanctuaries in the past, this process of quasi-sanctification is not surprising.

But as the trend for loft living has grown, drawing in more and more people equipped with huge financial resources for whom the loft is not a locus of actual artistic production but an essential fashion symbol, it is the minimal white surfaces of the art gallery that have increasingly informed the interior appearance of the modern loft. These 'curated' surfaces have resonances of purity, intellectual depth and calm detachment from the world, and they construct a space loaded with meaning. They are plaster smooth, and in covering up the tactile randomness of the traditional loft's brick wall (which you can alternatively sandblast to death), they provide a contemporary re-working of the *noli me tangere* construct, a metaphorical statement of the loft

5

dweller's enlightened, even transfigured status. With the distractions of the rough loft textures minimized, the narcissist is truly at home, being the only textured object visible.

'So many lofts are naturally introspective', says architect Mark Guard, whose exquisitely tailored lofts hide service areas, pull-out beds and hinged walls. 'The loft developer isn't interested in carving chunks out of a loft building in order to create balconies or garden terraces to give the resident some escape from the building. By not doing this, he can just say that he is maintaining the original character of the loft building, and the industrial brickwork is seen to be sacrosanct. Architects, I'm afraid, have also been responsible for creating prisons in these buildings. Even putting a "communal" garden on the roof is a sham. No one really wants to share a garden. They really want their own little patch of greenery', he adds. While a certain bohemian mess was one of the attractions of the early lofts, these white spaces instead suggest something of 'the anal clinician', to use Guard's description.

Lofts were once simple spaces: in fact, just simple space. As sanctuaries, however, they become paradoxes: refuge or prison? In his book *Minimum*, John Pawson has written that 'simplicity has a moral dimension, implying selflessness and unworldliness'.[15] It is 'a virtue that can purify the spirit and can offer adherents a sense of inner tranquillity'. But the fragility of this statement is evident when measured by Bachelard's contention, when writing of the protective model provided by the shell, that 'the imagination experiences protection in all its nuances of security, from life in the most material of shells, to more subtle concealment through imitation of surfaces. To be in safety under cover of a colour is carrying the tranquillity of inhabiting to the point of culmination, not to say, imprudence.'[16]

NOTES

1 _ Suzanne Slesin, Stafford Cliff and Daniel Rozensztroch, *The Book of Lofts* (Thames and Hudson, 1986) p. 113.

2 _ Gaston Bachelard, *The Poetics of Space*, trans. Maria Jolas (Beacon Press, 1964) p. 72.

3 _ Christopher Reed, ed. *Not at Home: The Suppression of Domesticity in Modern Art and Architecture* (Thames and Hudson, 1996) p. 16.

4 _ Reed, *ibid.*, p. 15.

5 _ Sharon Zukin, *Loft Living: Culture and Capital in Urban Change* (Rutgers University Press, 1989) p. 67.

6 _ *Ibid.* p. 80.

7 _ Wendy Moonan, 'Lofty ambitions', *House and Garden* (US), May, 1997, p. 114–125.

8 _ Zukin, *op.cit.* p. 80.

9 _ See Reed, *op. cit.* p. 15–17.

10 _ Jeff Wall, *Dan Graham's Kammerspiel* (Art Metropole, 1991) p. 50.

11 _ Wall, *ibid.*

12 _ Wall, *ibid.*, p. 52.

13 _ Wall, *ibid.*, p. 53.

14 _ Moonan, *op. cit.*, p. 122.

15 _ John Pawson, *Minimum* (Phaidon, 1998) p. 7.

16 _ Bachelard, *op. cit.* p. 132.

1 The loft at Neckinger Mills, showing the large table designed by Pimlott, and the orange wall of the kitchen area beyond, which lies beneath the beamed roof.

Southwark, London

Neckinger Mills

Mark Pimlott &
Peter St John
in collaboration with
Tony Fretton Architects

This loft, situated in the Neckinger Mills building in the Southwark district of London and 450 square metres (4,843 square foot) in size, was one of the first loft conversions in the city. Built in 1864, the building was used as a tannery until 1979. Designed in 1987 by Mark Pimlott and Peter St John, in collaboration with Tony Fretton Architects, the loft space was built a year later at a cost of about £170,000 for a record company owner and producer as a sole residence and workspace. The site was adjacent to a mass of railway lines on one side, and the shanty-town-like repair yards that congregate around the railway viaducts of London Bridge on the other. Pimlott explains that these elements of the urban landscape were 'a legitimate part of the city, whose value could be made visible through the design of an interior that was conceptually continuous with it. So, the loft was a big space with objects distributed within it as if within a landscape'. With the broad wooden floorboards acting as a flat terrain, the architects created volumes to signal the various functions necessary for the loft to serve as an effective living space: the kitchen area is seen as a coral-red rectangular block on the 'horizon'; the larder is formed out of a stainless-steel basket, its raw, porous grid pattern referencing the caged areas of parking lots, playgrounds and machine yards that are found in the urban landscape outside; the studio area – where the client might listen to music – is defined by mustard-coloured walls, and two large bookcases (one purple, one duck-egg blue) suggest the effect of aerial perspective upon vertical formations in the landscape. This is a loft that celebrates the chaotic epidermis of the city, a space that views the randomness of urban sprawl with optimism and even affection. It is, however, a very self-consciously theatrical environment, a stage-set version of the city: unreal, ideal spaces, places where the grime of true city life has been expunged or merely abstracted, a suggestion perhaps confirmed by Pimlott's view that 'we were very much making pictures with the work'.

But the architects were interested in making more than just a representation of the urban skyline: they were keen to examine how the textures and materials of the city assert themselves when subject to the inspection that occurs once these have been selected and abstracted within this loft space. Furniture

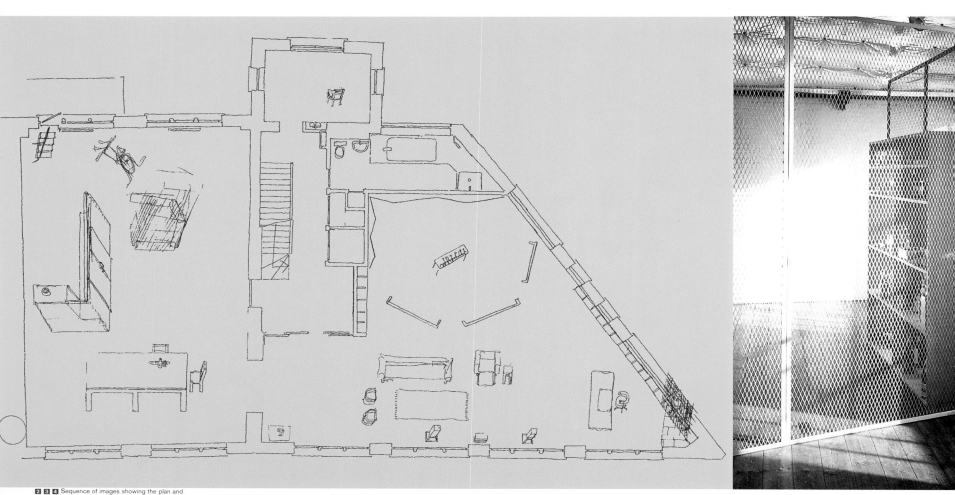

2 3 4 Sequence of images showing the plan and assorted views of the loft, including the wire cage of the larder and the open space of the seating area.

plays an important part in this process: Pimlott designed items to contribute to the picture-making of the 'scene' right up until 1994, with works such as 'Stair', which, in his words, is 'an escape stair, an occasional stair, rarely used. So it is designed to go nowhere, and it has no substance, only colour. It is a three-dimensional picture of a stair'. Then there is Pimlott's description of his 'Table': 'It's 3600mm long, so it comes in two parts. The ash component tends to accept work, while the sycamore component likes to be used for eating. This use is a happy accident of time'.

By producing an 'external' landscape within an interior space, the architects have emphasized the client's complete control over his world. It is an act not without its attendant ironies: acoustically, the loft insulates itself from its immediate surroundings – think of all those rattling trains – with sound-reductive flooring, insulated roof covering and firm double glazing. The loft is a floating world, in which the city's anatomy has been dissected and charted in beautiful lines and colours.

4

Borough, London

Culligan Loft

de Metz Green
Architects

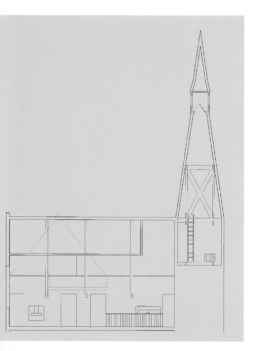

1

1 Long section (the spiral staircase going up to the tower is behind the section line). In the tower-bathroom, a series of original Victorian access ladders lead up to the crow's nest.

Young banker Susan Culligan's idea of the perfect loft is a secure and comfortable home that offers relief from the stresses of life in London's financial district. These high-ceilinged rooms, including a bell tower, perched on top of a nineteenth-century school building in south London are the ideal setting for her sanctuary.

The 139-square-metre (1500-square-foot) L-shaped apartment, completed in 1998, is made up of two former classrooms. Architects Julian de Metz and Amit Green have linked these spaces by creating window openings, doorways and a double-sided fireplace in the wall between them. This dividing wall, now rough rendered to signify its changed status, forms the spine of the apartment. On one side a vast space – complete with original timber trusses – contains the custom-designed kitchen, dining area, formal sitting room and stairs to the bell tower. In the 'snug' sitting room on the other side, a mezzanine bed deck has been slotted in with a bathroom underneath.

'The mezzanine is a new insertion so we wanted to do something that would contrast with the original space', explains Green. The result is the richly grained bed deck clad all over in cedar, a material traditionally used for garden buildings. The suggestion is of a scented bower into which Culligan can climb each night to sleep. Her four-poster bed, hung in white cotton, evokes further fairy-tale references.

Even more romantic possibilities are offered in the former bell tower, which de Metz Green have connected to the larger living room via a new spiral staircase. If, as de Metz suggests, 'living in a loft is about living somewhere special', then this tower is that 'special' element in Culligan's loft. A large bathtub clad in cedarwood stands in the centre of the room. Surrounded by windows but not overlooked, the bather has panoramic views over London in three directions. By climbing further up the tower, past a bed deck for guests, and out through a hatch, you reach the crow's nest. From here Culligan can survey the city, feel part of it and yet – from her lofty eerie – also feel secure in being far above it.

2

3

2 This top-floor loft, converted from old school rooms, provides the perfect urban sanctuary. The spiral stair climbs to the former bell tower – a fairy-tale Gothic structure – from which the owner can survey the City of London beneath.

3 Raised up on a scented cedar platform, a four-poster bed evokes further fairy-tale references (the *Princess and the Pea, Sleeping Beauty...*) that reject the urban nature of the loft in favour of more romantic associations.

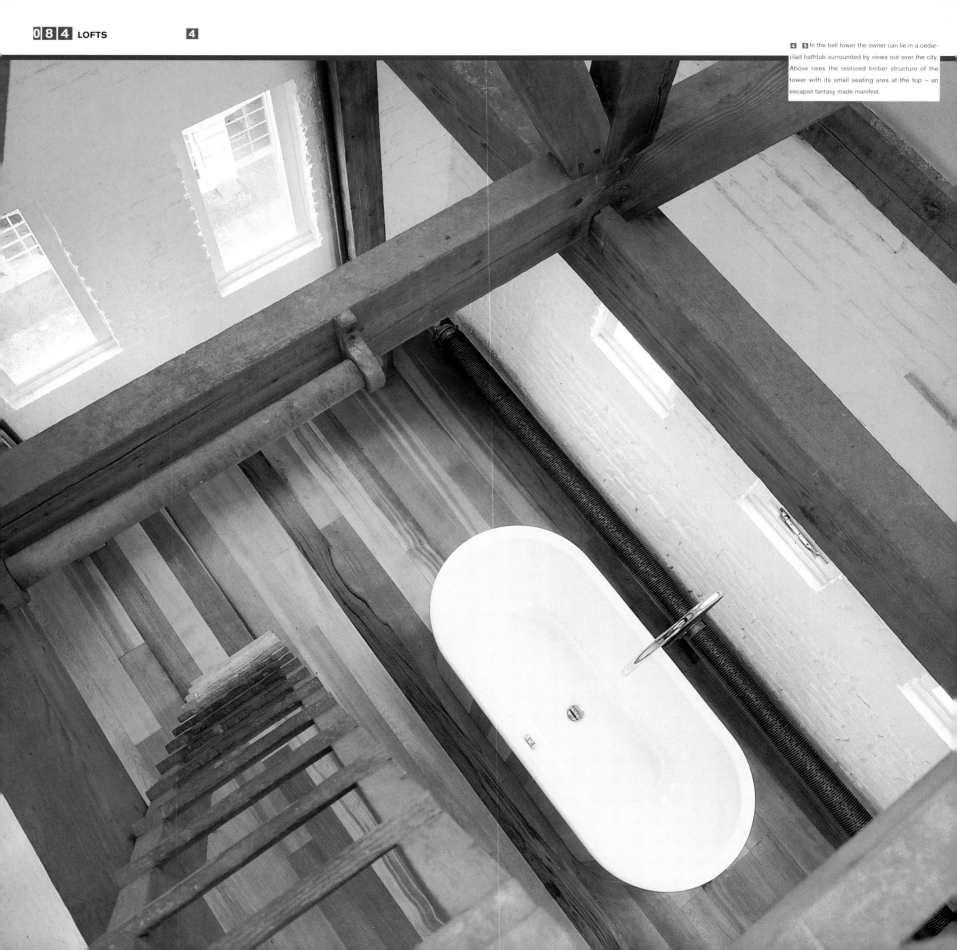

4 5 In the bell tower the owner can lie in a cedar-clad bathtub surrounded by views out over the city. Above rises the restored timber structure of the tower with its small seating area at the top – an escapist fantasy made manifest.

Hidden above the bustle of Neal's Yard in Covent Garden – a fashionable area of Central London characterized by a mix of chic restaurants, clothes shops and offices – this ingenious two-storey loft (completed in 1993) both celebrates its origins as a light-manufacturing unit and yet presents a luxurious hideaway for its owner, a businessman with interests in tourism and the media, who shares the space with his partner. Once inside the stark entrance hall – there is little to indicate at street level the existence of the loft above – the visitor is faced by a series of maple stair treads cantilevered off the wall, connected by an elegantly slim stair rail, leading to the loft above. The treads shorten as they ascend, increasing the sense of perspective. Grouped around the stairwell are a number of rooms serving different functions – utility and storage, two bedrooms, a bathroom and a separate sauna – that the architects decided could be placed beneath the larger open living space since they have less need for light.

On the floor above, the visitor is treated to a spectacular display of sculptural mass and volume: a series of curving dynamic walls wrap around the top of the stairwell – not gratuitous in nature, but rather a clever means of providing an energetic core to an existing awkward orthogonal space. Constrained by planning restrictions to maintain the pitched roofs on top of the warehouse, the architects installed a series of rooflights that unify the outline of the originally varying roof heights. With their dramatic sawtoothed silhouette, these rooflights reassert the light-industrial origins of the building. Elsewhere, the original steel columns supporting the building have been clad with plaster columns, but where these advance towards the ceiling, the cylinders have been cut back so that the steel beams inside can be seen, another reminder of the former rawness of the space. Within the open-plan living area, the architects have placed a perforated steel bridge that runs across from the dining area to the kitchen area, flanking a discreet study beside it. A cantilevered bar surface swings out from the kitchen area, and is made from Aerolam, a construction material normally

Covent Garden, London

Neal's Yard Loft

Rick Mather Architects

1 The staircase, cantilevered from the wall, soars
towards the sawtoothed roofline in two ascending
movements.

1

used in the aircraft industry, and serves as one of a number of floating horizontal planes on this floor that counteract the plunging diagonals of the roof.

As with many projects from Rick Mather's practice, access to a well-planned exterior space is important. Here, the architects have produced a garden terrace that is reached from the living area, but they have also ensured that visual connection can be made to other, smaller terraces from the bedroom and bathroom areas on the floor below through the expedient use of Privalite panels in the floors. These panels enable someone lying in bed, or in the bath, to look up at an angle through the floor above and out through a set of French windows on to an array of pots and flower beds – a visual access that negates the possible sense of enclosure but that can be controlled in turn and made opaque through a flick of a switch.

2 A view across the top floor of the loft, showing the breakfast bar, with its swinging aerofoil contours, past the kitchen on the left. The garden terrace is beyond.

2

5

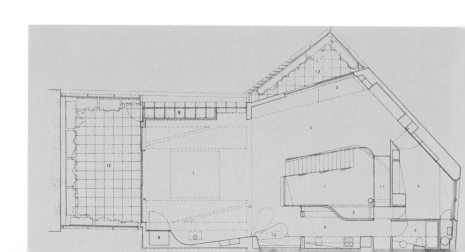

3 The central pillar beside the perforated metal bridge provides a dynamic accent to the series of folding curves and lines – a veritable piece of sculpture.

3

4 The top floor, showing to the left one of the glass floor panels, through which the visitor can peer down into one of the bedrooms, or conversely, up to the skylights above. Being made of Privalite glass, this visual access can be controlled by a flick of a switch, making the panel opaque.

4

5 Third-floor plan showing the roof terrace and living space. Around the staircase is the kitchen, with its aerolam table, and dining area.

6 Long section. The second floor comprises a large hall area: grouped around the stairwell is a utility room, bathroom with sauna and two bedrooms.

1 _ void
2 _ glass floor panels
3 _ dining area
4 _ study
5 _ bathroom
6 _ kitchen
7 _ living area
8 _ terrace store
9 _ service cupboard
10 _ aerolam table
11 _ steel bridge
12 _ roof terrace

6

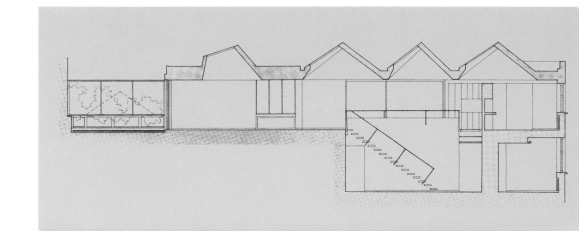

1 The boulevard, a quintessential urban experience in Paris, has informed the layout of this loft.

2 Plan of the Loft 'L', showing how the grid pattern or avenue of trees marries in with the living space.

1

Place Stalingrad, Paris
Loft 'L'

Pré-Saint-Gervais, Paris
Loft Wojciech Pszoniak

Alain Salomon Architecte

Loft 'L': This 278-square-metre (3,000-square-foot) loft, completed in 1997, is situated deep within the tissue of a residential block near the Place Stalingrad in central Paris. Formerly an atelier, or workshop, the building's light-industrial past has been well hidden from the public gaze, unlike American loft buildings that tend to be located right on the street line itself. The geographic enclosure of this French loft has influenced Alain Salomon's treatment of the space within it: as the architect explains, 'since there was little potential for an effective view to the outside and the client in any case didn't want to embrace a tough urban perspective, I decided I would control the client's engagement with what was going on inside the loft'.

To create this sanctuary within the city – and yet, paradoxically, distanced from its rougher textures and perspectives – an opening along the entire length of the back party wall of the loft was created, acting as a naturally lit canyon, bringing light to the dining and living spaces below. Most significantly, Salomon created an internal garden within the loft itself. This garden consists of twin rows of trees from the *Ficus* family, planted in a simple grid pattern. The trees are bedded in a vast concrete box set below galvanized metal gratings lying flush with the metal plank deck, and they are the subject of a set of internal views seen from a row of rooms – a library, guest/television room and a bathroom with a sauna, each with glass doors – located at the far end of the main living space. The trees are watered via an automatic sprinkling system and are covered by what Salomon terms 'sandwich plastic', which he chose instead of 'chic glass, in order to create a more industrial feel. I wanted the garden to be continuous with the hard surface of the loft, and achieved this by making sure there was no rupture in the space.'

In wanting his clients – parents of five children, two of whom still share the loft with them – to feel free to walk under the trees, Salomon has recognized the importance of the boulevard pavement experience so central to Parisian life and transposed something of its liminal, semi-park, semi-street status to the loft. There is also perhaps a hint of the French parterre indicated by the formal accuracy of the planting regime. It is tempting to suggest a further reference to Manet's 'Déjeuner sur l'herbe' of 1863, a painting that takes as its setting a picnic under the trees in a park.

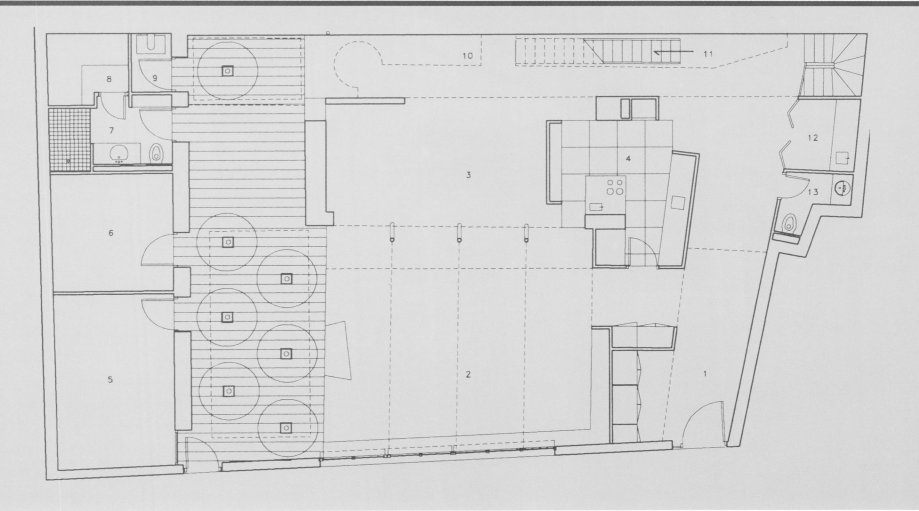

1 _ entrance
2 _ living room
3 _ dining room
4 _ kitchen
5 _ library
6 _ guest room
7 _ bathroom
8 _ sauna
9 _ boiler room
10 _ gallery
11 _ up to bedrooms and roof terrace
12 _ laundry
13 _ wc

2

3

Loft Wojciech Pszoniak: Located in the *banlieue* or outskirts of Paris, this loft building has been taken over by a community of artists and divided into smaller units so that each unit benefits from two double-height bays of windows. Salomon's clients, an actor and a psychotherapist, have no children and were insistent that the resulting loft space be as transparent as possible. The architect has installed a glass-block wall to form an envelope inside the loft around the bedroom and bathroom to achieve this. As an actor, the male client is familiar with the complex issues of representation and revelation, of masking and expressing identities, and his desire to obtain complete transparency of human function by requesting no visual barrier between the master bedroom and the bathroom – you can see everything in the bathroom – is certainly intriguing. The bathtub itself is made up of the same concrete as the floor.

The loft also houses an office for the female partner that occupies the basement level. Her clients enter on the ground floor and are met with the curving signature of a mezzanine wall above their heads, weaving its way inside the double-height space. A metal formwork ceiling runs throughout the loft, with vertical wooden beams adding contrast. As for the rest of the four-storey warehouse building, the residents were keen not to create isolated residential units, and so a set of wooden walkways and galleries were created inside the internal courtyards – now roofed over – in order to produce a series of linking streets between the various lofts that could not be 'privatized' by any one person. Judiciously placed pots of plants help to enliven these pedestrian spaces. 'This kind of project allows those who do not necessarily belong to an artistic community to adopt its lifestyle', adds Salomon, who continues, 'I believe the loft movement represents a special mode of gentrification of the city's industrial fabric, allowing enlightened people to share the artist's desire for non-conformism.'

4

5

3 Salomon has installed a curving mezzanine within the loft.

4 An exterior view of the Wojciech Pszoniak loft complex.

5 The bathroom of the Wojciech Pszoniak loft, which is open to the master bedroom.

1 MGA have designed this loft so that the volumes in the centre of the space appear to be sliding toward the viewer, and these are counterbalanced by the stasis of the long, panelled wall seen to the right.

Soho, London

Transformable Flat

Mark Guard
Architects

There was a time when a house told its story in passages that we, or at least our parents, knew well: entrance hall, reception and dining rooms, kitchen and utility areas, followed by bedrooms, which in turn would spawn a bathroom or two. But in the Transformable Flat, finished in March 1996 – part of the Soho Lofts complex developed by the Manhattan Loft Corporation – located in the eponymous district of central London, Mark Guard Architects have produced a multi-room apartment out of a mere 92 square metres (1,000 square foot) by implementing a flexible system of pivoting doors and moveable panel walls. A series of white panels runs down the entire length of the loft, their smooth surfaces unbroken by door handles. When, however, these panels are folded back, they reveal the kitchen area, all in stainless steel.

In the centre of the loft stands a set of rectilinear sculptural volumes, housing the bathroom – which consists of a stainless-steel bath and the custom-made glass cylinder of a shower cubicle – two lavatories and several hidden cupboard units. Further surprises are contained within the walls of this central structure: large panels hinge out to form a master and a guest bedroom – a sort of scene-making magic that enables the loft space to transform itself – hence the name Transformable – from a place where you could throw a casual drinks party for 100 into a small two-bedroom apartment. Fold-down beds concealed within these wall cavities complete the ingenious crafting. At the centre of this sculpture hangs a vertical sheet of Privalite glass that allows, at the flick of a switch, either complete transparency or opacity to the view out from and into the bathroom, bringing a *frisson* to the steel dining table that extends, like a catwalk, from the bath through the glass and out into the loft space.

The aesthetic rigour of the space – are these cuboid shapes an installation work in an art gallery? – is maintained by a pale cream limestone floor, white walls and grey metal windows. But while the clinical clarity of this loft represents a triumph of ingenious design over limited spatial dimensions, it is an environment in which the daily vicissitudes and mundanities of life have little place to be experienced. The panels yearn to be shut, the doors to be closed, the sculpture to assert itself. This is a show loft, a space to be displayed, a pied-à-terre perhaps, but not a home. Transformable and metamorphically brilliant. But never still.

2 The same space as the previous page, this view
shows the three panels enclosing the stainless-steel
kitchen folded back into their recess sleeves.

2

3 Plan demonstrating the transformable spaces.

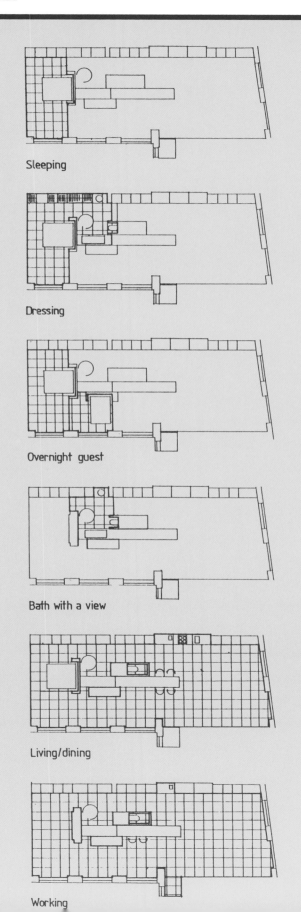

Sleeping

Dressing

Overnight guest

Bath with a view

Living/dining

Working

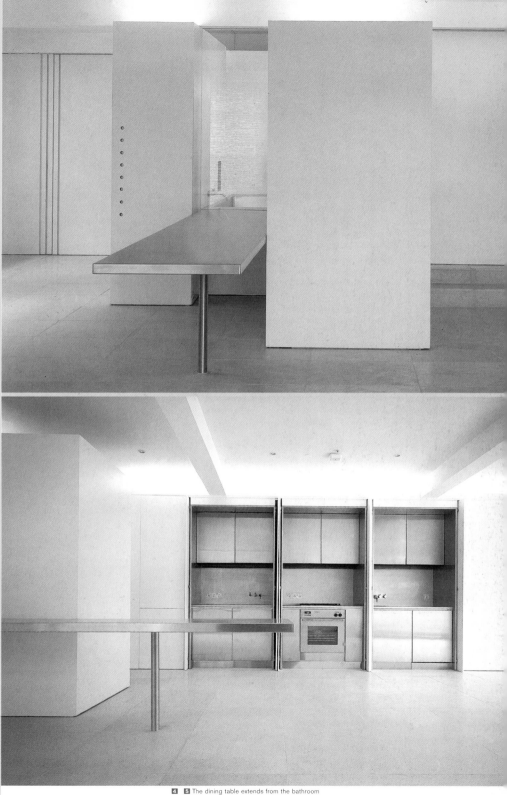

4 5 The dining table extends from the bathroom in a continuous run of steel, sectioned off by a Privalite sheet of glass that, when illuminated, turns opaque.

3

4 5

Lofts in Suhr, Switzerland

Ernst & Niklaus Architekten

Architects Bertram Ernst and Erich Niklaus have designed three lofts in a converted spinning mill in the northern Swiss town of Suhr. Their approach to each of the apartments – for a graphic designer, journalist and manager of cultural projects respectively – has been to give 'as much individual quality as possible at minimal cost'. Since the projects are interventions into an existing building, the decision has also been to 'accept the given on a small as well as a large scale'.

Inside the apartments, simple, modern materials and finishes (birch plywood, MDF, glass, stainless steel and aluminium) have been used to contrast with the original exposed cast-iron columns. New partitions are generally kept short of the ceiling to emphazise the building's generous volume.

The upper floor apartments have z-shaped plans. Here, a single piece of 'furniture' which touches the shell only at a few restricted points is used to contain and define the kitchen, bathroom, WC and wardrobe.

Although these slick projects are a far cry from the raw charm and experimental nature of early loft living in New York or Berlin, they nevertheless reflect a growing desire amongst the creative community in Switzerland to challenge conventional ideas of domestic space.

1 **2** **3** Views of the fourth and fifth floors of the former spinning mill in Suhr, Switzerland.

1

 The light-well and descending staircase of the Urban Interface Loft, as seen from the roof terrace. A sandblasted-glass light scoop above the living area transmits reflections of the rooftop cityscape into the living areas.

Duane Park, New York

Urban Interface Loft

Dean/Wolf Architects

The title of this project presents a paradox: situated on the top floor of a five-storey building in the Duane Park area in the middle of Manhattan, this loft, completed in 1997, brings together a set of linear and volumnar relationships that constitute an experience of the broader urban landscape. In the architects' own words, the Urban Interface loft 'can be seen as an idea about dwelling below a ground plane. The roof plane is sliced open to the sky, revealing the landscape of both the sky and its relation to the city. At the same time, the new urban ground plane drops into the centre of the loft.'

The paradox lies in the fact that Kathryn Dean and Charles Wolf have produced a space that suggests the subterranean, the hidden, the sacred even – in the way that a Pharaonic tomb is a ritually charged environment – on the top floor of a low-rise block in what must be, outside Hong Kong, one of the densest skyscraper forests in the world. Indeed, this sense of descent from the harsh external world into the reflective interior space of the loft is stressed by Dean/Wolf, who say that 'displaced and idealized, this new centre becomes a haunting space of slow passage'. Visitors enter a long hallway, lined by copper rectilinear forms to one side (are they sarcophagi?) and the eternal vista of a brick wall to the left. Copper is, of course, a material resonant with the glow of ancient cultures and suggestive of the subliminal electricity of healing properties. Their steps echo against the cooling, smooth concrete floor. They arrive at a central courtyard fringed with glazed walls, allowing them to proceed – at ritual pace – up the sheer-edge steps to what seems to be the roof of the world, where the panoply of Manhattan's straight-sided mountains lies before them.

Returning to the world below, visitors find that this glazed cuboid place is but a translucent space which, when viewed from inside, allows you to look straight through to the other side of the loft lying beyond the heavenward stairs. The glazed internal courtyard is, therefore, a temporary state of grace, an access for the spirit or *ka*, temporarily held within a terrain marked by earthbound ores and heat-fired brick clays. This is a loft where a sheer engineering precision and a clear delight in the cloistered use of light and the emotional implications of ascent and descent have combined to produce a space where luxury and liturgy work seamlessly together. The fact that the architects live here underlines how this project is not a showcase loft for a rich client: it is as clear a statement as they could make of their fundamental belief in the deep magic of the city, in the archaeological sensuality of its textures and materials, and, above all, in its power to act as the place where the human frame can be nurtured, protected and – dare one say it – even embalmed.

2

1 _ entrance
2 _ bedroom
3 _ courtyard
4 _ living space
5 _ office
6 _ light scoop
7 _ sleeping loft

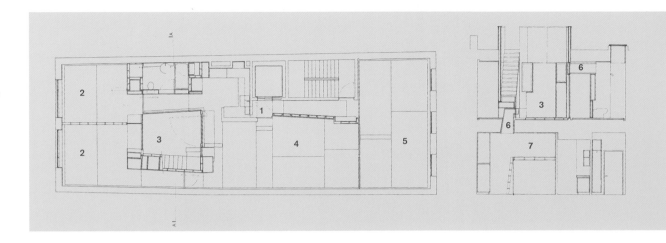

2 The courtyard area is cut out of the roof and looks towards the section of the loft designed to house Dean/Wolf's studio.

3 Plan and long section.

4 The long, tomb-like interior draws the visitor further into the loft's mysterious centre. Richly panelled sheet-copper is used to face the living-room partition.

3

4

Home and workplace

1 Home and workplace merged in the artists' ateliers of nineteenth and early twentieth-century Europe. Purpose-designed spaces like this Paris studio in the passage de Dantzig (artist unknown) from 1906, are in many ways the model for the first artists' lofts of 1950s New York (note the sleeping platform, now a feature of so many lofts).

1

'Early loft dwellers did not separate art from life', says New York architect and theorist Diane Lewis of the live/work culture that attracted pioneer loft dwellers to the big open spaces of Lower Manhattan. Among the primary attractions for these people – most of them artists – was the large amount of cheaply bought space offered by lofts as a combined living and working environment. This combination was clearly not a new phenomenon; it was the merging of work and life, claims Lewis, that made the artist's live/work environment different from operating a cottage industry, on the one hand, and the gentleman's study of history on the other. Lewis traces the live/work culture back to the artists' ateliers of nineteenth-century Europe where the painter or sculptor would sleep and eat in their studio. This model later became adopted across the Atlantic and, with the rise of Abstract Expressionism and Pop Art, led to a need for greater space to accommodate new, larger kinds of artwork. For the galleries that promoted this art, lofts also offered a dynamic and exciting environment for viewing.

As early as 1953, the 28-year-old artist Robert Rauschenberg was living in a loft in downtown Manhattan (the rent was just $10 a month). In 1960, the Pop artist James Rosenquist also took a loft in Manhattan, paving the way for one the most famous creative loft spaces of all: Andy Warhol's silver-painted Factory on East 47th Street, which reached its notorious peak during the sixties.

Through these precedents, the loft became the model for a creative way of life, for artists, writers, designers – and now new-media based businesses – where work and domestic life are one. 'You sleep late and you work late in a world unto yourself', says Lewis. 'The loft, with its

2

amazing dimensions, removed from the city and yet engaged with the city, becomes a formal symbol of that.'

The flexible form of the loft has developed to encompass many different types of work. What started life as factories, machine shops, printing works or warehouses in the early part of the century now supports new industries like marketing and digital design, in addition to the accommodation of traditional creative occupations such as architecture, photography and the music industry.

Architects Jane Tankard and Steven Bowkett designed their London loft as a live/work space (their planning consent from the London borough of Hackney demanded that some part of their space be dedicated to work). A totally open-plan space is the result, with desks and drawing boards in view of the bed, bath and kitchen. 'The idea', explains Tankard, 'is that you could have a bath and talk to someone sitting at a desk at the same time. It communalizes work.'

'In any job where you need space, the loft offers you the ideal place to work', says London architect James Soane who, with his partner Christopher Ash, started his architectural practice Project Orange from his loft. 'If you're setting up a business, the start-up costs are huge. It gives you the space to begin.'

'With lofts being urban, you have the advantage of location', says loft developer Harry Handelsman of the live/work ideal. 'You can have clients coming to you and you can reach everybody else.'

However, loft dwellers who live and work in the same space have not always been welcomed

by authorities or other businesses. 'Everybody lived and worked in the same place before 1927', says New York architect and loft dweller Henry Smith-Miller, who now runs his architectural firm Smith-Miller + Hawkinson from the loft he first occupied in 1972. 'Then, real-estate agents realized that if people had to live and work in separate spaces there would be twice as much real estate. So live/work is very frowned on by them.'

The occupation of commercial space for purely residential purposes has also been frowned on by authorities on both sides of the Atlantic. 'The cynical view of this', says Lee Mallett, journalist and former editor of *Estates Times*, 'is that the authorities who control these working-class areas want to preserve the existing political system so that they are able to stay in power.' In order to do this, the thinking goes, authorities refuse permission for residential use of industrial

buildings for fear that they may become gentrified and their traditional support lost. In practice, loopholes have been discovered in the legislation by loft dwellers. By arguing that their lofts will be live/work units and their buildings mixed use – often with shops, galleries, cafés and so on, at street level – many permissions for change of use have been granted. In London, precedents have been set that have then opened up whole areas for new loft development. However, in New York it is still illegal for non-artists to live in lofts in the SoHo district, a law which is aimed at maintaining the creative live/work culture of the area.

For many loft dwellers, from Germany and Spain to Brazil and the USA, the ideal of living and working in the same space remains. Siggi Pfundt, an architect in Munich, has recently designed and built her loft as a combined studio and home. Meanwhile, in São Paulo, Brazil,

4 The living spaces of Dieter Kramer's Kreuzberg lofts also comprised workshops.

5 6 Today, the changing nature of employment makes loft living/working the perfect solution for writers and academics such as Iain Borden and Jane Rendell, who is shown here working in their east London loft.

4

the architect and furniture designer Fernando Campana has converted a 1940s factory into his studio, workshop, showroom and home: 'the only thing rooted in the space is the ivy. This way I am free to transform the workspace into a home and vice versa.' In London, the artist Patrick Hughes still works in his loft, recalling the artists of the fifties, while interior designer Felicity Bell has recently fitted out her loft to accommodate her studio, meeting room and space for an assistant. 'Our work is such a part of our lives', says Bell, 'that it wouldn't be right to segregate it completely.'

The blurred boundaries between social space, private space and work space continues to be a defining feature of loft culture and an essential part of its complex nature. As Sharon Zukin writes in her history of the loft: 'Because it represents both home and work, hedonism and domesticity, and public and private space, loft living is paradoxical.'[1] So while the emasculated loft often portrayed by the media may be the shiny, clean apartments of bankers, lawyers or advertising executives, one of the fundamental tests of a true loft remains the same: proof that creative work goes on inside.

NOTES

1 _ Sharon Zukin, *Loft Living: Culture and Capital in Urban Change* (Rutgers University Press, 1989) p. 60.

5

6

São Paulo, Brazil

Campana Loft
Fernando Campana

According to the Campana brothers, loft living is a recent concept in Brazil, where designers have begun to revive buildings constructed in the fifties, sixties and seventies for domestic use. 'Here in São Paulo', says Fernando Campana, the Brazilian architect who, in partnership with his brother Humberto, is well known in the design world for thoughtful and often witty furniture products (several are now made by European companies, including Oluce and Edra Mazzei) 'we have very beautiful industrial spaces. Most of them are empty and falling apart; they were built in the beginning of the century by Italian immigrants. At times, the areas look like any suburb of Milan or Turin.' Located in wholly industrial areas, these structures suffer from a lack of basic services, such as transportation and commercial centres, and are often unsafe and solitary. Perhaps because of this, the loft culture in the main cities of Brazil – São Paulo, Salvador and Rio de Janeiro – is not normally centred around residential use, but mainly comprises restaurants, shops and clubs.

1

1 **2** Architect and furniture designer Fernando Campana has converted a 1940s former commercial building in São Paulo, Brazil, to make a studio, showroom and living space for himself. Such projects are rare in Brazil where loft living is a recent concept.

The Campana loft, completed in 1994, functions as a studio, showroom and living space. The 229-square-metre (2,464-square-foot) space occupies a former commercial building built in the 1940s in a residential district in central São Paulo. When Fernando Campana began work on the concrete-block building, it consisted of two parts, a front building linked to a back building via a lavatory block. From this original structure he has converted the ground floor of the front building to house a showroom/living room, the back building as a workshop/kitchen and the lower ground floor as a bedroom and bathroom. The linking lavatory block was removed to form a courtyard space.

To bring light into the showroom, a new full-height steel-framed window has been inserted into the back wall, over-looking the courtyard. Simple finishes have then been applied inside to maintain the raw feel of the building. The walls are roughly rendered and painted and the concrete floors have been burnt-waxed and polished.

Originally, Campana planned to use the space simply, as a prototype workshop and showroom. But once it was finished he decided he liked it so much that it would also suit his needs as a home. 'The only thing rooted in the space is the ivy in the courtyard', he says of the building's flexibility. 'This means I am free to transform it each day from a home to a workspace and vice versa.'

2

3

4

3 **4** A new steel-framed full-height window, reminiscent of the Maison de Verre in Paris, has been inserted to bring light into the sitting room/showroom. The walls are roughly rendered and the concrete floors waxed and polished.

5 The two buildings on the split-level site are divided by a courtyard. This lower area doubles as a workshop/kitchen.

5

'There is a lot of speculation about "loft living". It's a bit of a myth. We have designed a flat that happens to be in an old glue factory', says architect James Soane of the 92-square-metre (1,000-square-foot) apartment in east London that he and his architect partner Christopher Ash have designed for themselves in 1996.

Rather than take the bohemian lofts of New York as the only authentic models for this living-type, Ash and Soane have drawn on modernist principles and ideals of luxury as inspiration for their home. Describing the concept for their apartment, Soane has written: 'I like the idea of walking through the front door and pretending that it is a hotel room... To your left is the bedroom and to your right is the bathroom... The bedroom is very fitted... Very five star, very James Bond'.

Beyond a black pivoting door however, the apartment opens up to reveal a long, rougher open-plan living space with an exposed brick wall, metal factory-style windows at one end and a door on to a fire escape at the other. Behind a large sliding door is an office designed to double as the architects' studio and guest bedroom (the bed rolls out from the fitted storage wall). With the door open, the office flows easily into the living space, blurring the boundaries between work and pleasure, week days and weekends.

1 2 This apartment, carved out of a former glue factory in east London, is the home and studio of architects James Soane and Christopher Ash.

3 In plan, the progression of spaces runs from the entrance, past the private (bedroom, bathroom) area and the studio/guest room, to the large open-plan living room beyond.

Banner Street
Shoreditch, London

Ash/Soane Loft
Project Orange

1

The architects' treatment has been not to over play or romanticize the building's original features, but to leave them simply as evidence of past use. 'It has its own history written on it and you want to reveal that history', says Soane. A clear distinction has then been made between the gritty, original structure and any new insertions. 'For us, this is always to do with juxta-position, to do with "occupation" of space', he says. The result is a series of contrasts between the historic shell and the studwork and plasterboard construction, a floor in rough builders' ply and sleek contemporary furniture and fittings.

For Ash and Soane, designing and living in a loft is about freedom of choice, 'the ability', as they put it, 'to create an environment which is tailor made'. In their case, this means a modern, custom-designed space. But even they like to indulge in a little bit of loft romanticizing sometimes. 'In the summer', says Soane, 'you might like to think you are in New York, open the back door, sit on the black metal fire escape and drink a cold beer straight from the bottle.'

2

3

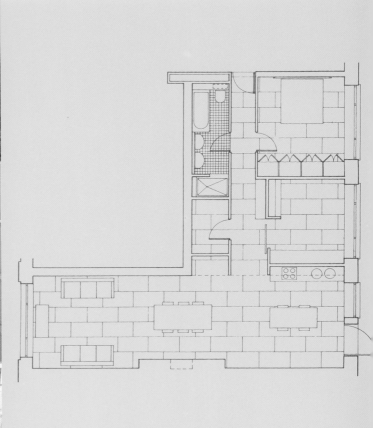

Munich

Pfundt Loft
Form Werkstatt

1 **2** German architect Siggi Pfundt has converted a space in a former sewing-machine factory building in central Munich to create a loft that functions as both her home and studio.

3 In plan, the loft is arranged with the main living space/studio running along the day-lit elevation, while the sleeping area and bathroom are planned to the darker, rear section of the apartment and are screened off by sliding plywood panels.

1

2

Five sliding plywood panels hanging from a steel rail in this apartment in central Munich separate the private spaces for bathing and sleeping from the main living and working areas. This inventive and flexible solution to partitioning is the work of Siggi Pfundt, architect and occupier of the loft, which was completed in 1997.

'In order to retain the original character of the former factory, the loft was renovated using simple materials and methods', explains Pfundt. The original concrete floor is painted in the living area, a custom-made stainless-steel unit functions as a kitchen and the bathtub is reclaimed from Pfundt's grandmother's garden. Other furniture and fittings in the apartment, including a sink, fridge, chairs and shelves, came from flea markets. The dining table is a dressmaker's table, an object found in the host building, which was originally built as a sewing machine factory. In the sleeping area, beech strip flooring has been laid to differentiate the space from the living room.

For Pfundt, the 70-square-metre (750-square-foot) loft functions as both a home and workplace. During the day the beech-faced partitions can be pulled back to create a large open-plan space with a working area at one end. At night these can be pulled across again to create a more intimate environment.

The most has been made of the modest DM30,000 budget for the project, with wit as well as practical considerations in mind. Evidence of this includes a ceiling for the lavatory cubicle constructed from wired glass, while a former dumb waiter has been converted, says Pfundt, 'into a sort of shrine/chimney ensemble'.

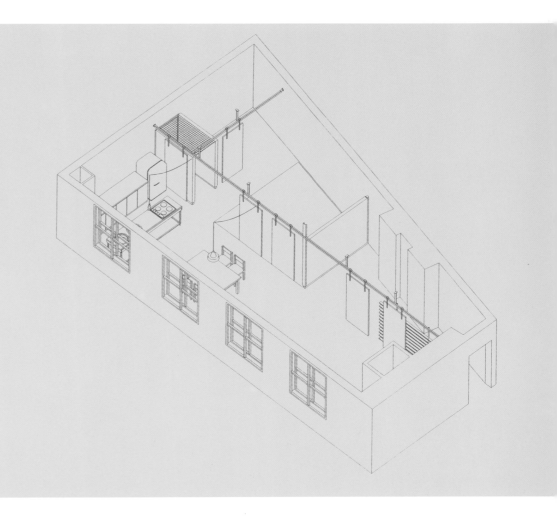

3

4

5

4 During the day the beech-faced partitions are pulled back to create a large open-plan living and working area.

5 Beyond the well-lit working area, the former dumb waiter has been converted, explains Pfundt, 'into a sort of shrine/chimney ensemble'.

6 **7** The screens separate the living space from more private areas for sleeping and washing. The furniture came from flea markets, while the stainless-steel sink unit is custom made.

6

7

1

Shoreditch, London

Hughes/Atkinson Loft

Willingale Associates
with Michael Green
of Green Homan

1 An exterior view of the Hughes Atkinson loft on Great Eastern Street in Shoreditch, London.

2 An intriguing view of the first-floor living space in the Hughes/Atkinson loft, showing the dining area and library. The white-painted timber floor is partially reflected in the mirror to the left, which throws light back into the space and complements the Philippe Starck chairs.

2

3 The artist Patrick Hughes and his assistant work on some paintings in the studio, which occupies the ground floor of the former polish factory.

4 Plan showing the position of the former director's room, whose entrance faces the kitchen/dining area.

3

This loft, situated within the Shoreditch area of east London, and completed in 1996, is the home and studio of the artist Patrick Hughes, who is known for his three-dimensional reverse perspective paintings, and his wife Dianne Atkinson, a historian. The 418-square-metre (4,500-square-foot) space occupies the basement, ground and first floors of a magnificent Victorian wood-polish factory constructed during the 1870s, which had suffered the indignity of suspended ceilings and hessian walls during its years as an office since the 1950s. As a live-work space, this loft has been at the vanguard of a growing reconfiguration of Shoreditch into a thriving creative-industries sector that has found a new lease of life in the many warehouse buildings in the area.

Entering at ground level, visitors find themselves in a totally white environment: the brickwork, plain panelled floor and slender cast-iron columns are all mere backdrops to the vividly coloured works waiting their turn on the many easels Hughes has erected around the space. A small library unit is located to the left, together with a kitchenette. Venturing down the white spiral staircase, the visitor comes upon an enormous basement art gallery, lit by a reveal at the front and artificial lighting elsewhere. The living accommodation is found on the first floor, and is lit by large southwest-facing windows. The floor is white painted timber, and the brick walls have been partially exposed. The kitchen, half hidden behind some storage cupboards as you progress through the space, meets

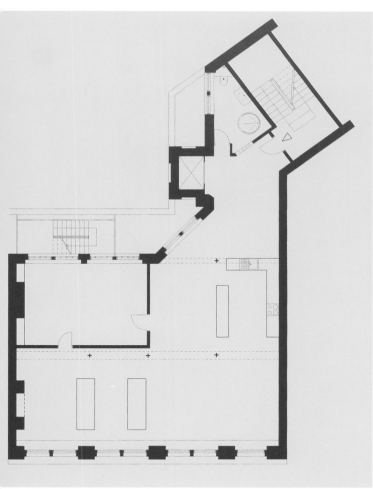

4

the dining area at right angles: beyond this there is another set of shelving units, followed by a small office space from which Atkinson works.

Philippe Starck door handles glint from the otherwise plain cupboard units. But the real surprise of the loft is the clients' bedroom, which is enclosed by the open space of the first floor and accessed through a discreet but solid door. Situated in what used to be the director's office, the bedroom is the only carpeted zone of the loft and has the original boardroom mahogany panelling on the walls, covered in the brown varnish that was the main product of the polish factory. The clients have decided to make a feature of this, and have retained one tin of the varnish as a reminder of the original purpose of this intriguing time capsule. Interestingly, by turning this office into their inner sanctum and using the lower floors as a working studio, the clients have maintained something of the zonal hierarchy that would have characterized the working regime of the original commercial inhabitants. The architecture of this light-manufacturing building, with its high ceilings and tall sash windows – which on the lower floors rise into bulkheads above the main ceiling heights – provide enhanced natural light over the whole floor area, thus making the loft a perfect workspace for Hughes and his assistants, who work with great concentration upon the artist's own architecturally ambiguous paintings.

1 An exterior view of the Nile Street loft building. The former garment warehouse appears much as it was earlier in the century.

2 The Rorrison loft looking from the kitchen through to the dining area in the main living space.

3 Axonometric of the Rorrison loft.

Shoreditch, London

Nile Street Loft 1
Tankard Bowkett

Nile Street Loft 2
Ken Rorrison Architects

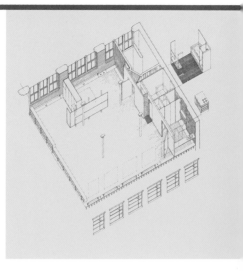

3

2

These two lofts occupy a former clothing factory in Shoreditch, in the London borough of Hackney. The handsome brick- and steel-frame six-storey warehouse was taken on by a collaboration of architects, designers and artists who all wanted a large space for both living and working that they could afford on an extremely limited budget. As a group, they acted as their own developer, architect and client. Use of the building was strictly limited to B1 (commercial/light-industrial) use and due to a glut of office buildings in London, it had remained empty and derelict for ten years or so. Consequently, the building was relatively cheap to purchase. The group was forced to take a huge risk by buying the building without planning permission to convert to live/work use, but after a year of negotiation with Hackney Council, a change of policy was adopted, which resulted in permission being finally granted. A factor in this decision was the presence of the famed Spitting Image modelmaking workshop in the other half of the building, which enabled the group to demonstrate that the building was already in commercial use. The residents moved in during late-1992/3.

Nile Street Loft 1: Jane Tankard – whose grandmother worked as a seamstress in the same clothing factory – and Steven Bowkett were keen to create a landscape of internal volumes which were influenced by that outside the building. They grit-blasted the walls, removing the fake wood panelling, and kept the old teak doors to the space. A series of shapes were designed to articulate the resulting space, the kitchen area consisting of three rectilinear tiered masses that do not extend their bulk to the ceiling. The concept of a bathroom was deconstructed so that a large white bath stands as an isolated block to the left of the entrance, fronting a larger white rectangular block behind which houses a lavatory and washbasin.

At the opposite end of the loft, two sleeping areas are separated by low walls – one for their young daughter, who loves playing in the empty and unrestricted loft – and one for themselves. A large work desk runs parallel to the massive length of original floor-to-ceiling windows that face the street. Two pairs of massive cast-iron columns give vertical lift to this emphatically horizontal terrain, continuing through the building, and becoming gradually more attenuated as they

4　　　**5**　　　　　**6**　　　　**7**

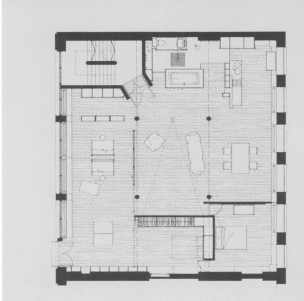

4 The Tankard Bowkett loft is perceived by the architects as a film set, with moveable elements within.

5 **6** Fixed elements, such as the kitchen units, or the bath, are treated as freestanding objects, in the architects words, 'like buildings within a landscape'.

7 The loft under construction in 1992.

head towards the small, but well-designed communal roof garden several floors above. Colour has been used with great care in this space, with different tones and values judiciously placed to suggest aerial perspective and distance. The fit-out of the loft cost between £15,000 and £20,000, including appliances: they were able to save on some of the carpentry costs by using the help of relatives to complete some of the work.

While the open-plan nature of the loft space has facilitated the application of an almost cartographical discipline upon the functional services essential to domestic living, both Tankard and Bowkett admit that it also limits the degree of privacy available to either of them when working from home. 'But that', says Tankard 'was a sacrifice we were prepared to make'.

Nile Street Loft 2: Ken Rorrison's 185-square-metre (2,000-square-foot) loft, a couple of floors above, similarly exploits the vast expanse of floor to good effect. However, he has avoided the creation of a separate bedroom space, including the sleeping area within the larger domain of the general living space. Instead, he has chosen to section-

off his kitchen – contained behind an orange panelled wall – and his bathroom, which has no external window ('an advantage, in fact, since it makes it a special zone, set apart from the openness of the loft', he says). Elsewhere in the space, Rorrison has used a fine external render on some of the brick walls for contrasting effect, and the familiar presence of the magnificent cast-iron columns supporting the building provides an apt metaphor for the sense felt by its inhabitants of their being part of a joint project. For Rorrison, the opportunity to create a living and working space in a loft was a distinct reaction to the claustrophobic dimensions of the Victorian housing he experienced when growing up in his native Scotland. But his move to this area of London, characterized as it is by many warehouse buildings, has not only enabled him to define his own sense of space in personal terms: he is one of the architects involved in designing the loft spaces in the development of the building opposite, a fact that neatly underlines the point that loft living often involves a blurring of the traditional boundaries defining where we live and work.

This ingeniously planned loft, completed in 1998 in the fashionable Clerkenwell area of London, is designed as a home and workplace for interior designers Felicity Bell and Christian Papa.

The intention was to retain the feeling of light and openness while at the same time creating areas for work and meetings which would not overwhelm the private nature of a home. The solution is a series of cleverly concealed sliding or folding screens which, when open, allow all the spaces in the apartment to flow into each other. When closed, the screens provide private areas for guests to sleep or for meetings.

'The appeal for us wasn't necessarily that the building was industrial', says Bell of the 1930s light-industrial host building. 'I don't feel that precious about it because it's not a beautiful example. If it was, we might have treated it differently.' Many of the original fittings, including the windows, have been removed over the years. Instead, the attraction of the 76-square-metre (820-square-foot) shell unit for the designers was the blank canvas it offered them to make a home perfectly suited to their needs.

Inside, the plan has been notionally divided down the centre with a partition that stands free of the external walls. This defines a large open-plan live/work area on one side and a bathroom and main bedroom on the other. Two screens in the entrance hall are normally pulled back to allow the space to flow freely into the living room. However, once a translucent glazed screen is pulled across, this hallway can be transformed into a meeting room. In this way, trade visitors never get to see beyond this defined area. A concealed door

from the hall opens into the bathroom to give these visitors access to a lavatory and washbasin, which can in turn be screened from the bathroom proper.

In another arrangement, part of the hallway/meeting room can be screened to create a guest bedroom. For this scenario, a bed and mattress fold out from the wall, the hall cupboard becomes a wardrobe and the door to the bathroom provides en-suite facilities.

In the main living space, one whole wall is fitted with a desk, shelves and space for a drawing board. This is Bell's studio, which can be closed off behind a folding screen in the evening or at weekends. 'Work is so much part of my life', she says, 'that it would feel like a waste of space to have a whole separate room for it.'

The sleek kitchen is planned along one wall with concealed rubbish bins and appliances. The richly coloured work surface is made of jarrah, a timber from Bell's native Australia (she trained at the technical college in Sydney). Throughout the apartment, the floor is in poured grey rubber, its highly polished surface appropriately matched to the slick nature of the apartment's detailing. Underfloor heating means that not even radiators intrude into the calm.

Like many contemporary loft dwellers, Bell and Papa have furnished their home with classic modern furniture (the dining table and chairs are by Charles and Ray Eames, as is Bell's desk chair). This choice reinforces the theory put forward by many loft dwellers that such apartments represent the continuation of Modern Movement ideals of domestic space.

Clerkenwell, London

Rosoman Street Loft

Felicity Bell

1 The original structure of this slickly detailed London apartment, the home of designers Felicity Bell and Christian Papa, is concealed beneath a poured-rubber floor and suspended ceiling. Rather than emphasizing the former industrial nature of the space, the shell has been conceived more as a 'site' for a new apartment.

2 **3** The hallway functions in three ways: as a hall, a guest bedroom (the bed folds out from the storage wall), or as a meeting room for Bell and her clients.

1

2

3

4 Bell's studio occupies an end wall in the living space, with built-in storage and mobile tables.

5 The studio can be screened off at weekends or in the evening leaving the Eames chairs to become part of the living-room furniture.

7 8 A series of translucent screens divide the hall from the living room. Here, the hall is in meeting-room mode. With a bed folded out from the wall, the space becomes a guest bedroom.

6 9 10 In plan, the apartment is ingeniously conceived to make maximum use of the space. The lavatory is accessed from either the main bedroom or from the hall. This allows it to be used by trade visitors (when it is screened off from the bathroom), guests (when the hall becomes a guest room) as well as by the occupiers themselves.

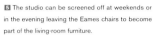

4

5

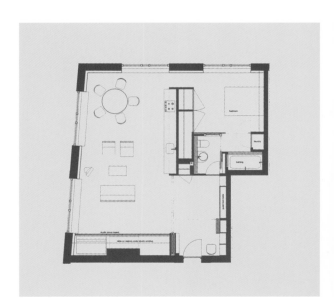

6

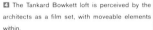

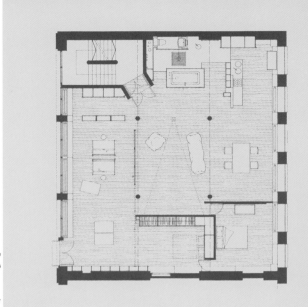

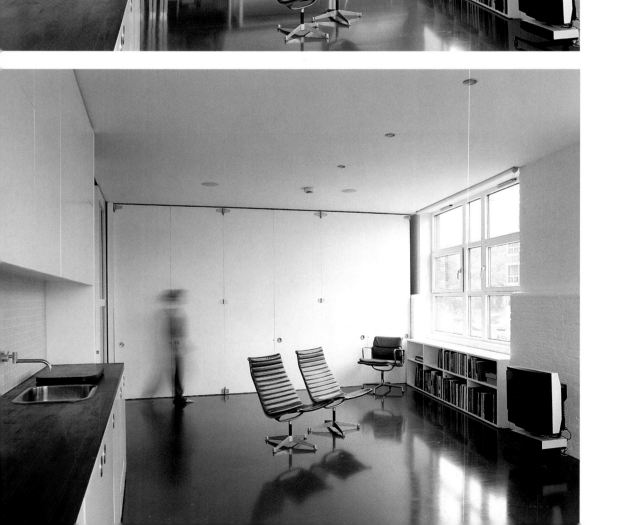

4

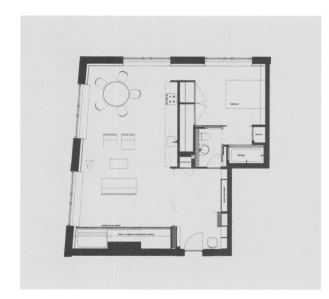

6

5

9

7

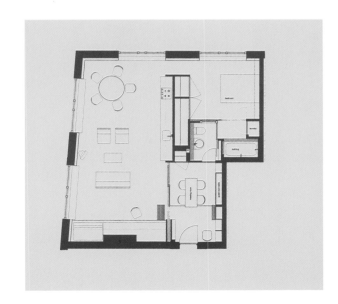

1 0

8

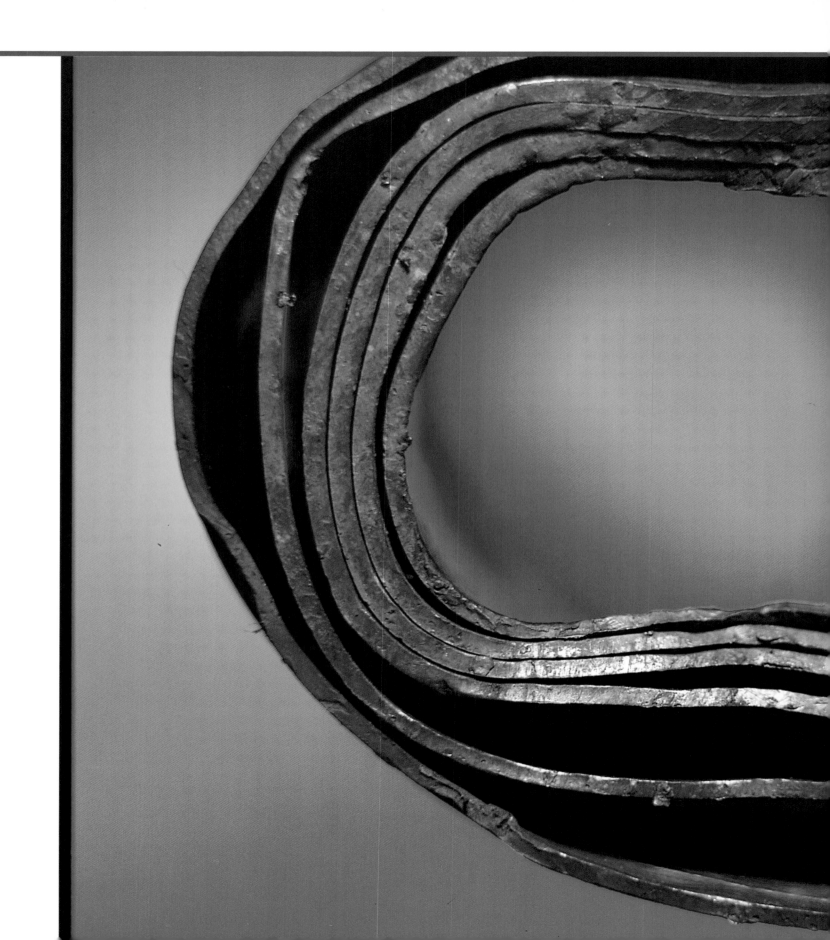

Detailing and fetishization of objects

A loft, in the original sense of the word, deriving from the United States, simply means an upper storey of a warehouse or factory. More specifically, the word now conjures up an image of a converted open-plan space in which the original structure is juxtaposed with new architectural insertions and evidence of domestic use. For Sharon Zukin, chronicler of New York loft culture, the description of the archetypal loft is clear-cut:

'While loft buildings are constructed on a comparatively small scale, their proportions are generous. Usually they have five to ten storeys, with 2,000 to 10,000 square feet of space on each floor. Older loft buildings have only a freight elevator, but newer ones also have passenger elevators. Ceilings are high – 12 to 15 feet – and are supported by either vaulted arches (in smaller buildings) or columns. Architectural detail is often classical, reflecting late-nineteenth-century taste for the Italian Renaissance. Columns in loft buildings are frequently fluted, and the building façades are generally cast iron, which marks an important innovation of the time in the industrialization of construction technique. In contrast to the construction materials used in modern buildings, those used in loft buildings are more solid (brick and iron) and more valuable (often oak flooring and even copper windowsills). Because loft spaces are indeed "lofty", they offer the potential for drama in everyday life. Lofts are good for exhibiting large works of art, using professional stoves and refrigerators, luxuriating in mammoth whirlpool baths, and experimenting with an avant-garde *mise en scène* or decor. In short, lofts present a perfect setting for gracious late-twentieth-century living.'[1]

This image of the loft, with its giant windows and minimal partitioning, has become peddled the world over through films, magazines and other media. But in addition, certain materials, finishes, furniture and fittings have become de rigueur in loft culture and a language of description has even developed.

A list of loft 'must haves', published in the UK-based, mass-circulation *Mail on Sunday*'s *You Magazine* in April 1998 illustrates the point. It said:

'Loft-dwellers love: glass bricks; stainless-steel fixtures and fittings; the adjectives raw, urban, vibrant and challenging; metal beams and sandblasted walls; Conran sofas with curved backs; pale wood flooring, particularly ash and light American oak; the phrase "soft modernism"; long thin cylindrical radiators; and underfloor heating.'[2]

A particular palette of materials and a certain way of furnishing has become the acceptable, even clichéd, way of fitting out a loft. But for some, this denies the true origins of loft culture, which is often considered to be about providing the freedom to live however you choose.

For Manhattan Loft Corporation chairman and developer Harry Handelsman, the freedom of the empty shell is still the greatest asset offered by loft living. 'At our first building in Summers Street, there are 23 apartments and about 12 distinct styles', he says. 'Some of them are fitted out like country homes, but that's fine. Flexibility is the essential ingredient of a loft.' Having said this, Handelsman does draw the line at some things. 'What would annoy me is curtains', he says. 'We put a clause about that in the contract because it would ruin the look of the building outside.'

For architects like James Soane of Project Orange, the argument is less clear. 'You have to decide whether to take a moral stance on it', he says. 'It's a shame when people create a suburban setting in a loft with a three-piece suite and wallpaper. If an architect gets involved in a loft it should be more than the suburban house. It becomes gymnastic, like a 3-D puzzle.'

1 The now-familiar image of the loft is of a vast open space which offers the potential for drama in everyday life. Key signifiers of 'loftness' include expressed structure, industrial materials and oversized furniture and fittings (including sports equipment more usually found out of doors). Shown here is a loft studio/home for a musician and producer in Jersey City, New Jersey by architects Abelow Connors Sherman.

1

2 Loft dwellers and architects search out what they consider to be appropriately industrial materials – for this SoHo loft, Moneo Brock Architects have used chipboard – for use in loft interiors.

3 Bicycles, propped in entrance halls or hanging from walls or ceilings, have become one of the hackneyed signifiers of the self-conscious loft dweller determined to subvert traditional images of domesticity by bringing outsized, outdoor objects into the interior space.

4 A loft designed by Alan Buchsbaum in New York in 1976. New insertions, such as the glass-block screen, floor tiles (that also cover the bed base) and a mirrored closet are juxtaposed with original, almost decaying elements, such as the wood columns, strip lighting and Anaglypta.

2   **3**   **4**

Ralph Ardill, a director at the London creative consultancy Imagination, agrees. Interviewed about his loft in Clerkenwell by London's *Evening Standard* in 1996, he said: 'Some people miss the point of loft conversions, and immediately they get their hands on one they put in three bedrooms and two bathrooms. Here, there's a stainless-steel kitchen in one corner, two Le Corbusier sofas, a Japanese-style bedroom, a workplace and a bathroom, which has a concealed door for when people stay. I have four girders', he continued, 'which I've painted purple, and [have kept] all the original graffiti from the nineteenth century.'3

Meanwhile for Tyler Brûlé, editorial director of *Wallpaper* magazine, the loft conjures up a cross between the Pop Art culture of the sixties with a bourgeois nineties love of industrial-looking appliances. 'Behind closed doors', he said in the *Mail on Sunday*'s *You Magazine*, 'you can

pursue a Warholesque notion of living in your own Factory. So much of our culture is, after all, about playing out lifestyle fantasies... There's a big element of "Look what I've got: a 14-foot ceiling and a stainless-steel Bulthaup kitchen."'4

London architect Steven Bowkett would rather do almost anything to provide private spaces than partition up his loft. 'It's always a struggle, detailing the loft to keep the spirit of the big space', he says. 'But I'd rather buy a shed from B&Q or a caravan and dump that in the space than make lots of bedrooms. If you try to impose the system of the house on the loft, you're going to run into problems.'

New York architect and long-time loft-dweller Henry Smith-Miller tells a story that he uses to illustrate what happens when the modern spirit of loft living is crossed with an inappropriately

suburban sensibility. To counter the cold of the vast space, his former flatmate hung velvet curtains at the windows and built a bedroom pod in the middle of his loft with its own air-conditioning. 'I think they were trying to create a Regency-style apartment or something', recounts Smith-Miller. 'But then one night there was a bang and lots of dust in the street and a huge portion of their ceiling had fallen in. I think the loft was getting back at them.'

Malcolm Holzman, a New York architect and loft dweller for over 20 years, agrees. 'If you're going to live in a loft, it's ridiculous to chop it up and make it into an apartment. My son rides his in-line skates [here] and we can have 100 people to dinner sitting at tables. That's the beauty of it.'

Responding to the prevailing attitude to the loft as a hybrid of industrial space crossed with contemporary domestic space, designers and dwellers have developed a range of architectural moves and a palette of materials that are now widely considered appropriate. The established approach is that original features and materials should be left exposed. It is in this way that the popular image of raw brick walls, stripped-back columns and timber floors has developed. Into this raw space a number of interventions can then be made.

In large-volume loft spaces, one of the most practised architectural moves is the insertion of a mezzanine, usually for sleeping. This loft staple has obvious origins in the storage mezzanines of warehouses, but more particularly, explains New York architect Diane Lewis, in the artist's ateliers of turn-of-the-century Paris. These light-filled purpose-built apartments provided height for large canvases and a small mezzanine space for the artist to sleep. The form of this space

became associated with creative achievement and established a model on both sides of the Atlantic. Then, as Lewis says, 'intellectuals wanted to live in them too'. Modernist architects, led by Le Corbusier, developed the idea. As time went on, says Lewis, 'the Abstract Expressionists took this model and moved it into the loft', and the precedent was established. Now, often devoid of this historic context, the mezzanine is most used by developers as a way of adding 'visual interest', and gaining more space and thus value. For architects and occupiers, the mezzanine is simply as another familiar symbol of 'loftness'.

Once the plan and structure of a loft is complete, the business of finishes, fittings and furnishings comes into play. Most architects working on loft projects take the approach that materials and finishes should reflect the industrial origins of the building. As a result, a number of appropriate (but nevertheless stereotypical) fittings and finishes have developed as part of the language of loft living. Among these are the stripped wooden floor (sometimes solid or original, often a laminate imitation); stainless-steel kitchen and bathroom fittings and appliances; industrial light-fittings; and radiators. While architects and loft dwellers take great delight in sourcing new or second-hand fittings genuinely intended for industrial or contract

use (hospital taps, prison WCs and heavy-duty flooring are among the most popular), many of the fittings made to look industrial have now been developed by suppliers with the particular intention of servicing the loft market.

Despite protestations from loft-lovers of the freedom offered by this domestic form, it is remarkable how tyrannical some can sound about appropriate furnishings for these spaces. As Ralph Ardill's earlier comment about his Le Corbusier sofas illustrates, classic modernist furnishings and their more economic contemporary substitutes – usually by Conran, Habitat or IKEA – have become staples of the loft look.

For Diane Lewis, there are clear reasons for this association. She sees the development of the loft in the direct lineage of the Modern Movement quest for a democratic and new way of living. As she says of her designs for apartments: 'There are no walls in my projects that are just walls. They absorb objects so that the space is left and you have a place to dream'. While some might see the results as austere, Lewis suggests the potential that the environment offers for 'peace inside, while you feel the city as a landscape around you'. To reinforce these modernist principles, she has furnished her loft with classic pieces by European exponents like Gerrit

5 In Mark Guard's Transformable Flat, conventional forms of furniture are challenged by a table that travels on tracks across the open-plan space.

6 Because of its converted status, the loft form often challenges designers to find new ways of solving problems. In Resolution: 4 Architecture's Potter's Pad of Planes, in New York's Chelsea district, light is bought into the kitchen and dining area via a series of 20 carefully composed bars of light, linked to four dimming controls that can be individually adjusted to suit the mood of the client.

7 The Meisel loft from 1979 flaunts its size through its display of various large-scale artworks, a refectory-style dining table and billiard table. The open-plan organization of space, together with the Eames lounge chair and ottoman refer to the loft-type's Modern Movement roots.

7

Rietveld and Eileen Gray and the later American interpretations of modernism by designers like Harry Bertoia.

Although their intentions may be less cerebral, other loft dwellers and developers have adopted modernist classics such as Le Corbusier's leather and chrome chairs, Arne Jacobsen's famous ply dining chairs and Alvar Aalto's bentwood chairs as loft favourites. There is nothing original in this. As James Soane comments: 'From all the possibilities that exist for reinventing the way we live, people still paint everything white and buy a few well-chosen clichés as furniture'. But in many of the more interesting loft settings, these 'clichés' sit alongside shabby but comfy finds from markets (sometimes even skips), which are deemed acceptable and appropriate because their roots lie in the bohemian loft movement of the fifties and sixties.

Certain other symbolic objects or possessions have become associated with the lifestyle of the loft. The mountain bike or gym equipment strewn about the loft are de rigueur in marketing material, while signs of the wilfully undomestic, things normally too big to have in the home or more normally associated with outdoor pursuits, are often included – like pinball machines, basketball nets, swings, roller skates, table tennis tables or furniture of outlandish proportions.

As loft living continues to grow and spread across the world, these images shift and are reinterpreted by different cultures. In a Helsinki loft, the light fittings are by Aalto; in Barcelona, the colours of the loft become richer, the furniture made from rattan and leather; and in São Paulo, the loft is furnished with Brazilian artefacts from the fifties and seventies, as well as pieces by the loft dwellers' own company, Campana. Like all the artefacts of cultural production, lofts are not free-floating, but rooted in the particular time, place and socio-economic group of their inhabitants. As the projects on the following pages illustrate, loft style is subjective. Despite the clichés, the answer to the question of 'what is loft style?' remains the same: it is whatever you want it to be.

NOTES

1 _ Sharon Zukin, *Loft Living: Culture and Capital in Urban Change* (Rutgers University Press, 1989) p. 2.
2 _ *You Magazine, Mail on Sunday,* 5 April 1998.
3 _ *Evening Standard,* 28 August 1996.
4 _ *You Magazine, op. cit.*

1 Matteo Piazza's photographs of the apartment he occupied in 1978 reflect his romantic ideal of the bohemian loft. The freestanding bath in the open-plan space is a classic detail of early loft culture.

1

Union Square, New York

Matteo Piazza Loft
Matteo Piazza

Matteo Piazza, the well-known Italian architectural photographer, has very romantic memories of the New York loft he occupied during the summer of 1978. 'I was 18 years old and I had just finished high school', he remembers. 'By chance I saw a sign in West Broadway from someone saying that they would lend out their loft rent free if the tenant would fix it up'. Piazza took up the offer and moved in.

'The building was on Union Square, but it's been knocked down now', he explains. 'The door had the sole of a shoe hanging from it and the first floor was a boxing den. It was like being in a movie with Al Pacino. You could smell the people fighting'.

Inside the loft, Piazza found a big run-down space with steel columns, a wooden floor and a roll-top bath standing in the corner. 'I cleaned it up, fixed the electricity and painted it. You can see the green colour I chose on the bath', he says. 'All the things I used in the loft were objects I found there'. These included the wooden palettes and garbage cans that formed the bed, and the oar adapted as a lamp stand.

Now based in Milan, Piazza looks back on his time living in a loft in New York as a formative experience. 'I came from Trieste, which is very provincial', he says. 'It was the first time I had lived on my own and I played basketball every day in the square'. Even now, despite being in a different city and in a different time, loft living still influences his life. In his large 100-square-metre (1,076-square-foot) Milan home, for example, he has no doors. 'I like open space', he says. 'The idea of that loft is still the idea of my house'.

2 Most of the furniture and fittings in the loft were found by Piazza on the site and adapted for new uses.

3 **4** With a typical loft dweller's resourcefulness, an oar has been adapted as a lamp base while garbage cans function as a bed base.

2　　　　**3**　　**4**

electricians, steel-welders, plasterers and such like, applied their aesthetic understanding to the practical jobs in hand. Community spirit very much defines the prevailing ethos of this loft, and it is interesting to note how this and the nave-like space reminds one of the grand communal endeavours to build the leviathan cathedrals of the past.

Lewis explains how 'the large-scale corporeality of the factory building and its surrounding Brooklyn neighbourhood of brick towers and almost Pasolini-esque Italian atmosphere gave the project a church-like ambiance from the outset', and this has directly influenced the reductive logic of the loft's plan. This sensitivity to the Italian tradition and the shapes and perspectives of the Renaissance is further highlighted in a quirky feature of the design: sited at the opposite end of the loft from the porthole aperture of the elevator door is another porthole viewpoint that pierces the external brick wall. The object of this second peephole is to frame the slender hyperdermic silhouette of the Chrysler Building, that iconic heart of the Manhattan skyline. Lewis describes how this intriguing aspect came about: 'rather than making this view, which was never seen before, promiscuously accessible, I decided that it should be more secretive. In doing this I was directly influenced by a circular hole built by Piranesi – who isn't really regarded as an architect – into the wall of his church on the Aventine Hill in Rome. This view frames the dome of St Peter's, and is an obvious tribute to that great building'. By framing the Chrysler Building in this way, Lewis has provided a scintillating view across the urban skyline and has demonstrated how the physical entity of that building can transmute into an imaginary version of itself, at one time pictorial and iconic. Peepholes, portholes and gaps in buildings create inevitable *frissons* for both the observer and the observed: such lines of sight fetishize both the object and the space from which they operate, and in this, both the Chrysler Building and the loft itself are subject to a privileged, but respectful, gaze.

5

1 Concealed behind this modest and unassuming building in the financial district of Manhattan is a slick, nineties take on the bohemian loft of the sixties.

1

Financial District, New York

Ron's Loft

Resolution: 4 Architecture

A far cry from the bohemian origins of New York loft culture is this interpretation completed in 1997, where the building's industrial past is almost entirely concealed beneath a slick skin of architectural details.

The third-floor 518-square-metre (1,700-square-foot) apartment in the financial district of Manhattan was originally fitted-out for the client in the early eighties. When Resolution: 4 Architecture came to look at it with a view to redesigning the kitchen, they proposed instead a complete remodelling of the apartment to open up its 'loftness'.

In order to create an open-plan volume – traditionally the defining feature of a loft – the architects straightened the sides of the long, narrow space where the lift and stair towers previously projected inwards. This straightening has been achieved by packing-out areas along the sides of the space and adjacent to the lift. These new boxed-out areas contain two bathrooms and a series of storage solutions, from wardrobes to bookcases.

The long swath of ordered space created in the centre of the loft has been divided largely by use, rather than by physical partitions. At the rear of the loft is the sleeping area. A new bed, specially designed by the architect, is cantilevered off a slab that doubles as a headboard and, on the other side, a back plate to the cooker. This monolithic structure, say the architects, is conceived as the 'hearth' of the home. The progression of spaces runs from the bedroom, through the kitchen and dining areas, to the sitting area and finally to the work and guest rooms at the front of the apartment.

What makes this loft interesting is its complex and carefully considered details and its unusual palette of materials. Rather than overtly expressing the loft's industrial past, the portions of exposed brick wall have been concealed under white paint. Elsewhere, new partitions for bathrooms have been clad in a composition of Durock insulation panels. The ceiling is also clad in insulation panels and above the living area these have been built up in a sculptural composition of layers.

The highly polished and smart appearance of this apartment is completed by furniture specially designed by the architects. This includes the coffee table, the dining table and the kitchen island unit (a rectangle, a circle and a square respectively). A cocktail table on castors has been custom-designed in stainless steel for the kitchen. Overall, the effect is of a high-class, glamourous urban style, which has become associated with a certain kind of bourgeois nineties loft living.

2

3

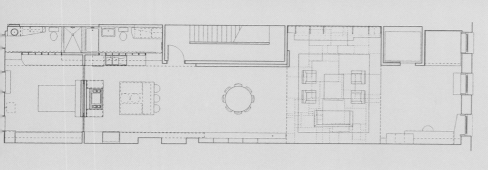

2 **3** The refurbished apartment represents a luxurious ideal of loft living with furniture, including a cantilevered bed, specially designed for the space.

4 Plan of the third-floor loft renovation. The existing long, narrow floor area has been divided up into zones, from front to back, as office, living, dining, kitchen and sleeping.

5 Despite the slick detailing, the architect has still left some original fittings exposed as token credentials of loft authenticity. The now-hackneyed cliché of a wall-mounted bike suggests a knowing reference to loft culture.

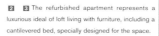

4

5

Poble Nou, Barcelona

Vapor Llull Lofts

Cristian Cirici & Carlos Bassó

1 The 100-year-old Masso i Carol chemical factory in the Poble Nou district of Barcelona is the city's first major loft development. New lift towers have been added to the front of the building to mark its change of use. The 'B' signals the ground floor, 'M' the intermediate floor, and 'S' the top floor.

2 The 18 lofts in the building have been finished to shell standard, leaving buyers to fit-out their own spaces.

3 The former factory has been cleaned and painted and new glazing panels installed.

1

2

3

4 This engraving of the Isaura metalworks in Barcelona from 1877 records the presence of Barcelona's thriving industrial heritage, before companies moved out to the city's outskirts.

5 Inside, the newly fitted lofts show a diversity of approaches, but many of them reflect a traditional Spanish sensibility and choice of materials. This space is for an Egyptologist, who has kept the open-plan arrangement of the loft, while creating a double-height space.

4

5

'We have been persecuted by the authorities', says architect Cristian Cirici of the trouble that has erupted over what he claims is the first loft development of its kind in Barcelona. Completed in 1997, the project is the conversion of the 100-year-old Masso i Carol chemical factory in the Poble Nou industrial area – on the coast, close to the 1992 Olympic Village – into 18 loft apartments.

Since the building is situated in a part of the city that is zoned for industrial use, the authorities have not yet officially recognized its status a residential development. 'One day the police came to take pictures to show that people lived there', explains Cirici. 'It's like New York in the 1960s when it was dangerous to live in lofts.' Despite this current situation, the architect thinks it won't be long before the authorities agree that developments like this are a good way to regenerate the city's declining industrial areas. 'They are considering how to solve the problem. It is a very popular discussion in Barcelona', he says.

The factory had long been disused when the architects discovered it. 'It was a complete mess when we bought it', remembers Cirici. 'There was one main building and the rest of the space was just full of obsolete structures. We tore these down and just preserved the basic building.' In addition, the 30-metre- (98-foot-) high tower of the former steam turbine house has been retained 'as a symbol of the time when the entire Poble Nou was full of steam-powered industry'.

Cirici and Bassó's treatment of the building has not been over reverential. To mark the change of use inside they have stripped its original render and painted its brick walls with vividly coloured silicate-based paint. Three tall lift towers have also been added to the front of the building, each clad in enamelled corrugated steel, like a giant silo. This finish, combined with the big painted apartment numbers, gives the towers an appropriately industrial look.

The 18 apartments, each around 90 square-metres (968 square-feet) in size, have been sold in shell form, allowing the final occupiers to design their own interiors. On the lower floors, the units come complete with the original steel beams and vaulted ceilings exposed. On the top floor, the dramatic timber trusses of the original structure remain intact.

For Cirici, the development of these lofts reflects the significant changes in Spanish culture that have occurred since the death of Franco. 'The people who live in them are not people in a standard situation', he explains. 'They are singles or couples without children. This is a new situation in Spain, so I think lofts are going to be quite popular.' The attraction for these pioneers, says Cirici, is the large volume offered by the 5 metre- (16 metre-) high ceilings. 'If you buy a 100-square-metre (1,076-square-foot) apartment in the city, it has four bedrooms, two bathrooms, a kitchen, a hall, a living room and a utility room. But if you are single why do you need four bedrooms? People like the freedom to use the loft space as they want.'

Another factor in the success of the development, says Cirici, is the changing nature of work and the blurring of boundaries between home and office. Many of the new loft dwellers also use their spaces for working, mostly in creative professions. 'Like President Clinton and Monica Lewinsky', suggests Cirici, 'there are things that are traditionally done in the home which are also now done in the office.'

As to the future of lofts in Barcelona, Cirici is convinced that the phenomenon will take off. He has recently completed the conversion of another factory and thinks more will follow. 'People are waiting for it', he says. 'The problem is that the legal situation is not clear enough. Once they allow that to change I think that people will begin to develop lofts.'

6

7

6 Loft of the architect Normand Cinnamond, a large space containing an eclectic mix of furniture and souvenirs.

7 The minimally styled loft of young architect Inés Rodriguez allows her to lead a versatile life in a large neutral space.

8 Plans: ground, intermediate and top storeys. The carparking space is a rare luxury in Barcelona. The tenants of Vapor Llull were looking for an alternative space than the traditional four-room, two bathroom apartments.

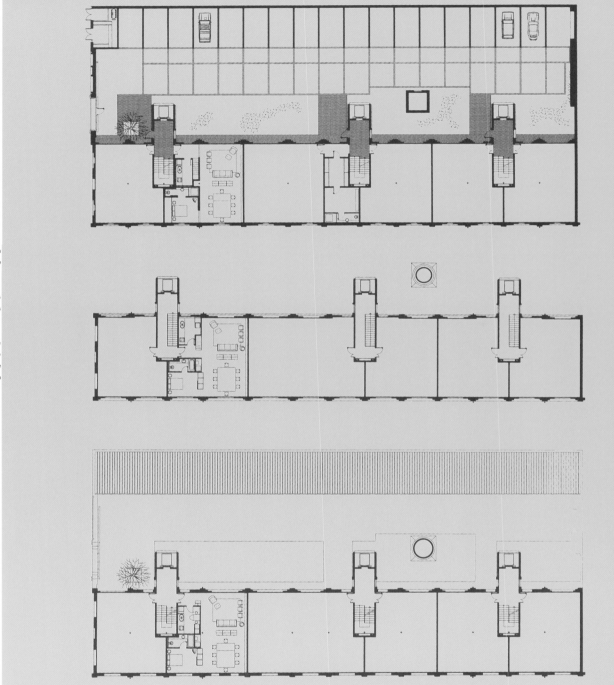

Image: the role of the developer and the media

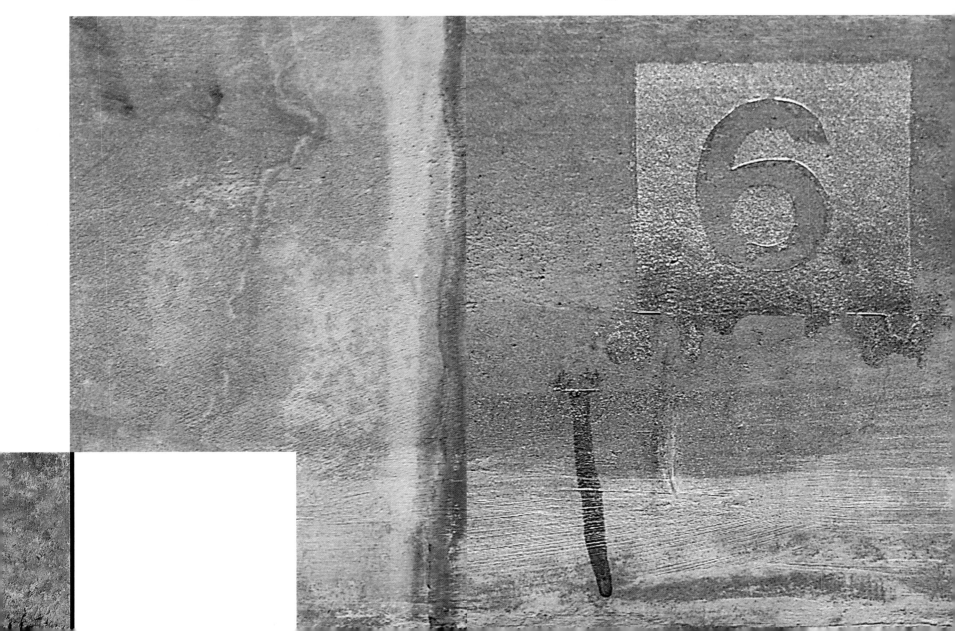

The role of the developer in shaping the worldwide loft phenomenon (as well as the urban landscape in general) cannot be underestimated. Developers deserve credit for rescuing dilapidated loft buildings and bringing out their potential, and for providing numerous architects and designers with the chance to produce novel and exciting work. They have given a small, but influential clientele the ability to choose how they design and live in their own space. On the other hand, some developers have exploited loopholes in planning regulations to create living spaces in warehouses that have unsuitable standards of acoustic protection, external aspect, and internal configuration. Developers have also been known to quote unrealistically (but conveniently) low figures for the cost of fitting out a shell in order to sell the unit. But the most significant aspect of the developer's role is the fact that it is they who create the markets for living spaces and it is through them that a specific kind of language is developed to describe the value of those spaces to their consumers.

It is hard to pinpoint exactly when developers started marketing loft living, but by 1975 loft rents in New York City, running at an average of $400 a month, had become as competitive as rents for a standard three-bedroom apartment, then ranging from $350–450 a month, despite the fact that living in lofts in the city was, until around 1975, illegal.[1] Nonetheless, the marketing strategies that have subsequently dominated the selling of lofts around the world had by then been well established.

The development of a wider market for loft living in the early 1970s resulted, as Sharon Zukin has observed, from a change in value-perception. 'Sweatshops existed for many years, and no one ever suggested that moving into a sweatshop was chic.'[2] 'On the one hand,' she goes on to say, 'artists' living habits became a cultural model for the middle class. On the other hand, old factories became a means of expression for a "post-industrial" civilization. The supply of lofts did not create demand for loft living. Instead, demand was a conjunctural response to other social and cultural changes.'[3]

[1] The Manhattan Loft Corporation, probably the largest loft developer in the UK, has transformed several former industrial sectors of London.

1

While the first loft-dwellers had, in the main, been engaged in the creative arts, owners of loft buildings soon realized that they could market the image and ambience of the brilliantly expressive artist to members of the public who had little or no direct involvement in the arts world. This use of cultural capital to reach and influence new audiences mirrors, albeit in miniature, the CIA's support for the global dissemination of Abstract Expressionism during the fifties and sixties in order to promulgate the image of the United States as 'the vigorous world power'.[4] From their original function as sites of light-manufacturing production, to their role as sites of 'artistic' production, these lofts thus assumed a further role as psychologically dynamic spaces in which the loft buyer, so the developers' marketing brochures claimed, could express and fulfil their personality.[5]

In New York, developers could use the media profile of artists already resident in lofts in midtown and downtown Manhattan (SoHo, Tribeca, Chelsea) and the waterfront areas of Brooklyn as a means of promoting the contemporary appeal of loft living. In cities elsewhere in the United States, the term 'New York-style lofts' has been used as a way of branding the old industrial sectors with desirable urban chic and arty associations.[6] However, in America's deep south, Diane Baker, a realtor with Gilman International Holdings Ltd of Atlanta, Georgia, observes that lofts are referred to in the current marketing literature as 'historic or turn-of-the-century' buildings. They are 'completely restored', or have undergone 'retrofit', have been 'rediscovered', are ready for 'adaptive re-use' and 'reflect the original beauty of years gone by'. As with loft adverts generally, much emphasis is made of exposed brick walls, beam construction, ductwork and sprinkler systems, original hardwood or factory-style (sealed concrete) floors, high ceilings and huge factory windows with spectacular city views. While they are often fitted out with 'European' or 'Euro-style' kitchens, these lofts are 'a one-of-a-kind opportunity. Unique. Not your typical "cookie-cutter" condominium'.[7]

In London, which, at the time of writing is the main focus of loft development in Europe, developers often use – with apparently little awareness of the ironies at play – the term 'New York-style lofts' as a means of promoting the authentic urbanity of loft living. The corporate logo of one of the largest loft developers in the UK, Manhattan Loft Corporation (MLC), who pioneered the British loft market with projects in Summers Street, Clerkenwell, and Wardour Street in Soho, is an intriguing example of geographical schizophrenia, with its amalgam of the twin towers of New York's World Trade Center, London's Canary Wharf and other assorted landmarks. As Harry Handelsman, chairman of MLC explains, 'When we developed the concept of lofts in 1992, it was quite new to London. In order to make it more accessible, a number of explanations were required. Our lofts had to be promoted in a manner that emphasized the possibility of creating your own space. The message is simple: if you want to create your own identity, then we can do it for you.'[8]

The double-page colour photograph in MLC's corporate brochure describes this identity: boldly framing the image is the massive tower of Bankside Power Station, now the Tate Gallery of Modern Art. From here, the potential loft-buyer is presented with a panoramic view across the River Thames towards the gleaming towers of the City, London's financial heart and the place from which many of MLC's clients earn their living. This is a perspective that the residents of Bankside Lofts – the corporation's most ambitious conversion/new construction project to date – will soon enjoy. The deliberate positioning of the client's viewpoint, with its subtle coupling of commerce and art, persuades the buyer that while they are tigers in the boardroom, they are aesthetes when at home.

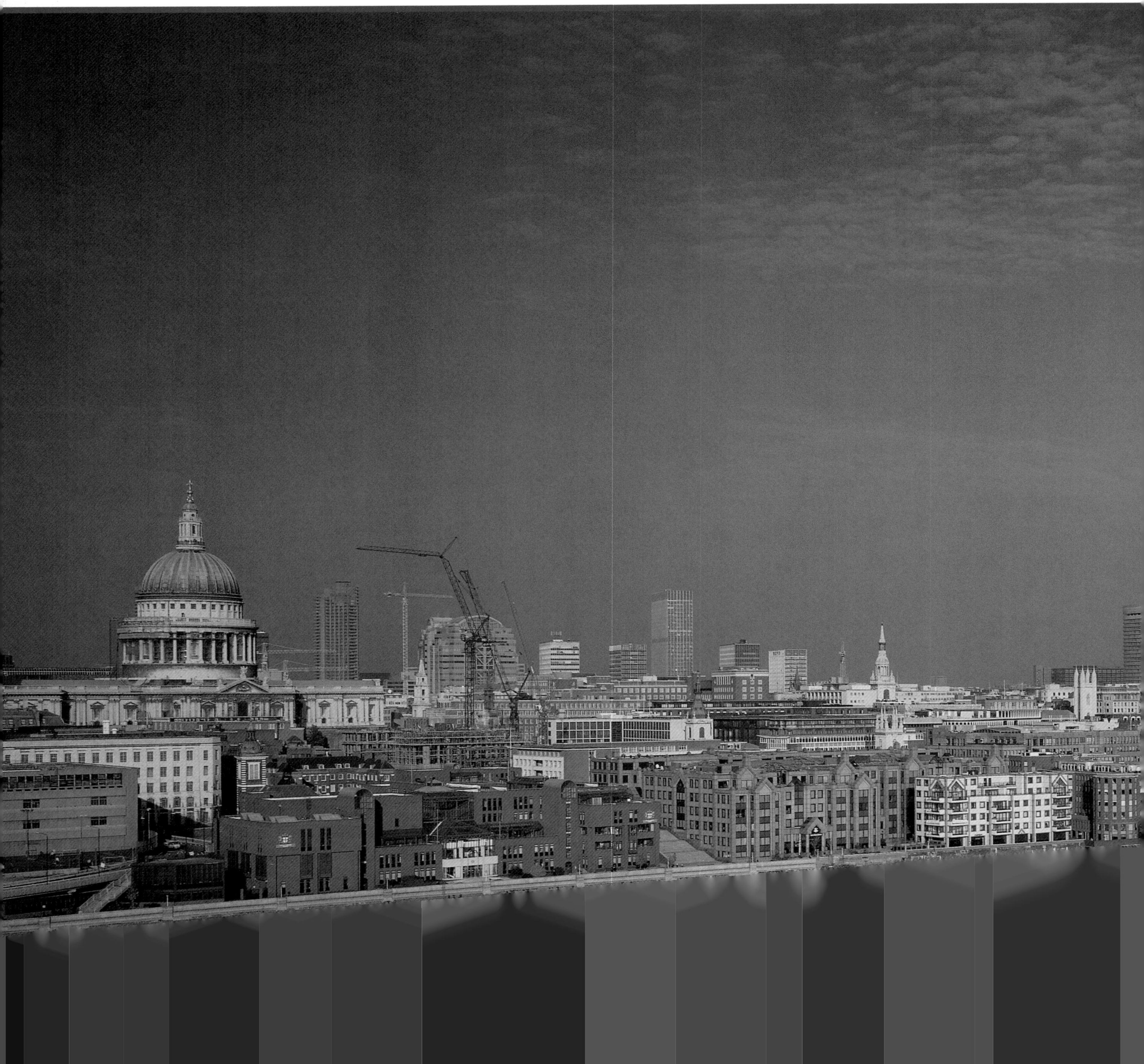

This magnificent panorama of London occupies the centre spread of a Manhattan Loft Corporation brochure. Asserting the value of urban living against suburbia, the image is one of regeneration and renewal (note the tower of the former Bankside Power Station to the right, which will house the new Tate Gallery of Modern Art).

The loft purchaser's arty credentials are heavily underscored in the marketing literature for The Factory, another MLC project in the Shoreditch area of London. The loft complex owes its name to Andy Warhol's eponymous and ultra-hip New York headquarters, and the client is helpfully reminded in the brochure that the look was 'driven by a more extreme aesthetic, plumbing was left deliberately exposed, walls left raw, a factory feel deliberately cultivated'. In a vague compression of logic, the reader is told 'the artistic legacy remains, with over 10,000 working artists residing within 2 square-miles [of Shoreditch], creating one of the most authentic loft schemes this side of the Atlantic'. On another page, the reader is confronted with the optimistic statement taken from the fashion magazine *Harpers & Queen* that 'people who live in lofts are tougher, innovative and artier, prowling the metropolis in search of more and more unusual places to put down roots'. These bold statements are accompanied by paeans to urban living from respected design names such as Eero Saarinen and Richard Rogers; a reference to the local residency of British artist Rachel Whiteread (a Turner Prize winner); close-ups of Mediterranean food; and blurred photos of people in restaurants. Artist and architectural theorist Mark Pimlott believes the frequent use of this type of blurred image, with its almost fetishized abstraction of the sorts of objects commonly found in Habitat catalogues and other design-conscious publications, together imply a 'dreamspace' of fashionable necessity that the viewer is compelled to enter.[9] Carefully interwoven into this lifestyle packaging are the inevitable grainy black-and-white photographs of loft buildings in their pre-renovated, decrepit state, their noble industrial façades seen in magnified blow-up: a wealth of design opportunity awaiting the intrepid loft-buyer.

The casting of the potential loft dweller as art genius and frontier explorer is further stressed in the brochure for MLC's (unsuccessful) plans for a loft development at 42–44 Sackville Street in Manchester: 'each of these spaces is a virgin canvas waiting for the occupant to shape and furnish it to their own needs and desires'. But this breathless prose is surely outdone by the phrases that adorn a photograph of a run-down warehouse interior used in another of MLC's brochures: 'You make each one unique'; 'You are in control'; 'You can do whatever you want'; 'You can have whatever you like'. The image climaxes with the blunt conclusion: 'You end up with more personality'. One is reminded of Samuel Johnson's conclusion that 'promise, large promise, is the soul of an advertisement'.[10] But then again, the marketing is clearly working: according to Handelsman, MLC has experienced a nine-fold increase in profits and turnover over the last six years. When asked by MLC to submit some ideas for a loft scheme in association with Harper MacKay Architects, Pimlott provided a not dissimilar, but profoundly ironic list of statements, this time crafted as if spoken by the loft dwellers themselves. The repeated use of the word 'like' – with the bland mediocrity that it implies – is exactly the point: it emphasizes the way that mobility, supposed cultural sophistication and a need to be at the forefront of fashion, have all become necessary elements in the merchandising of 'lifestyle' as 'the ultimate commodity'.

You make each one **unique**

90/10 "I am quite happy that 90% do not understand lofts, so long as they are endorsed by 10%."
HARRY HANDELSMAN Manhattan Loft Corporation

19/10/1998 15:58   4040057   CALMANN & KING LTD   PAGE 02
13/10/1998 16:11   0181-987-0256   MARK IRVING   PAGE 02

You
are in
control

You can do
whatever
you want

You can
have
whatever
you like

You end up
with
more personality

We like to keep on the move.

We put things where we can get at them.

We have all kinds of pictures and books.

We like to live simply.

We like to always feel as if we have just arrived.

We do what we want to do.

We like the city.

We enjoy being busy, and we enjoy relaxing.

We like pleasure.

We like to feel as if we can just get up and go.

We like to get up and out.

We like to be at the centre of things.

We like to feel we do what we want to do.

We like to feel on top of things.

We like the idea of being like artists.

4

5

4 The Manhattan Loft Corporation provides a lifestyle manifesto for potential buyers.

5 A fax from the architect and artist Mark Pimlott to the *Lofts* authors, listing the text he submitted to MLC when, in association with architects Harper MacKay, he was requested to provide a design for a loft space.

furnish your loft in one of **3** ways

ART
GLASS
TABLE
CHAIR
SOFA
RUG

6

The hypnotic egomania of MLC's 'You' list (is it surprising that, in Handelsman's own words, MLC 'has not had much success in selling lofts to couples with young children'?) is matched by the pseudo-Zen tutorial of Warner Lofts' brochure for its development in London's Clerkenwell district: 'The Paramount Building, early morning. The view from up here takes the breath away. The silence, and the cool air of the new day provides a necessary moment of calm, a sensation of timelessness, that permits proper mental preparation for the challenges of the day ahead in the transient, hectic city below'. (One can imagine the keen-jawed financiers – those 'Masters of the Universe' in Tom Wolfe's *Bonfire of the Vanities* nodding sagely here.) 'To live like this in the midst of the city is to constantly cross the threshold between public and private, between calm and chaos, between thought and action. Just appreciating this helps us to grasp the limitless opportunities that urban living can offer. The challenge is to always use this knowledge creatively and profitably. (Who said interior design couldn't bring you spiritual wisdom?)

But these 'limitless opportunities' can be problematic. 'Many people just don't know where to start when furnishing a loft – particularly if they have moved from a more conventional space', says Orianna Fielding Banks, owner of Pure (the name hints at the sacred status of interior design), an interior design business that specifically targets the loft dweller.[11] She has created a ready-made 'Loft Pack' consisting of out-sized pieces of furniture that 'have been designed to address the difficulties in scale that are often presented and offer a visual "one-stop shop" for all the essential elements of urban living'. Her marketing brochure provides the loft dweller with a helpful diagram showing him or her where to put the various items of furniture. But, she warns, 'this is not investment furniture. It's theatrical and people will probably want to remodel their interior and change it in three years'. *Sic transit gloria mundi.*

The exportation of loft culture lock, stock and barrel to other European cities has met with some limited success, and has been influenced by the varying nature of the urban physiognomy and cultural attitudes in each city. In Paris, for example, MLC has chosen to develop existing non-industrial buildings in the Marais district, aiming instead 'to introduce a contemporary lifestyle formula to traditional French homes based around courtyards'. In Berlin's Kreuzberg area, developer Paul-Lincke-Höfe's largest loft project, designed by Christoph Langhof, is configured around a series of internal courtyards that echo the prevailing plan format in Berlin for residential apartment blocks, but has in addition five 'Paradise Gardens' (created by US landscape designer Martha Schwartz) arranged on the rooftops – for use by the loft-dwelling immortals. While the project's sales brochure is free of the slick lifestyling common to those in the UK, it nonetheless draws on a composite iconography of both American and British features to sell the glamour of loft living to the German public: there's the photograph of Andy Warhol on the set of *Camp* at The Factory; the show flat (oddly enough, a

6 A page from Pure's marketing brochure, which shows clients how to furnish their lofts.

7 Paul-Linke-Höfe's Kreuzberg development, before construction. The former factory site stands between the Reichenberger Straße (left of the picture) and the canal (right). The Kreuzberg factory buildings were formed around courtyards.

8 9 Paul-Linke-Höfe's 'Loft-Leben in Berlin' project. The Berlin-based developer has used a photograph of British architect Allies & Morrison's project for the show loft, to the lower left.

10 A collage of marketing images, where the loft dweller is portrayed as someone with the potential to relate to the street and its bars, cafés and taxis, and yet who will also be able to assume a view from on high, with its dissociation from the dreary mundanities of daily life.

London loft by British architects Allies & Morrison); the 'vital' accessories of loft living – the grand piano, specifically featured on the loft plan, the Australian tree fern, the stage lights, the fine art rug. There are even pictures of London's Big Ben, New York's Statue of Liberty and a black-and-white photograph of an American milkman.

Lofts have also served as marketing vehicles for other products in numerous magazines and on television. They have served as regular settings for absurd fashion shoots in style magazines such as *Wallpaper**. In a 1987 television advert for the then Halifax building society, we were presented with the vision of a hunky account executive in his over-decorated warehouse loft going through the usual Sunday rituals before leaving to get money from the conveniently close cash-point machine. By 1988, loft-dwellers were already being satirized in the Holstein Pils advert, in which a stubble-jawed man wrests a car seat from a scrapheap and turns it into a reductionist artwork in his loft to the approval of his tight-lipped 'muse'. The whole process is justified by the use of Mies van der Rohe's motto 'less is more', which appears at the end. The die was fully cast by 1996, with the black-and-white Cussons soap advert that depicted a humourless dysfunctional couple inhabiting a

grey minimalist loft space, their inner emotional lives only enlivened when, in each other's absence, they can enjoy the sensual qualities of a bar of soap.

In films, lofts have provided rather more sophisticated metaphors. An example from 1981 is Jean-Jacques Beineix's *Diva* where M. Gorodish spends time exercising his elusive character in a *louche*, but oh-so-sophisticated warehouse space fronting the river in an unspecified Paris location. Early loft signifiers on the set include the Vietnamese character Alba roller skating across the expansive wooden floors, and M. Gorodish sitting in a steaming-hot free-standing bath in the rugged, open-plan space.

The psychotic protagonist of *Fatal Attraction* (1987), Glenn Close, lives in a downtown loft, approached through steaming sidewalks, a steel door and clanking lift, which symbolically contrasts with the married couple Michael Douglas and Anne Archer's uptown apartment and cute New England country cottage. The loft is where the dangerous liaison takes place: it is the zone of the anti-family, the liberating, illicit moment. The warehouse loft is the venue for another adulterous encounter in *A Fish Called Wanda* (1988), albeit rendered extremely comic. The loft-dweller-as-

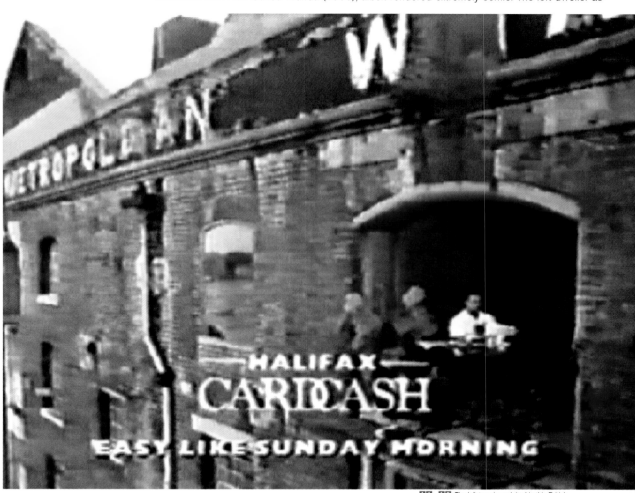

11 **12** The loft-type is exploited in this British television advertisement from 1987 from the Halifax building society. The loft-set is surrounded by the gritty urbanism associated with loft living.

13

artist is explored in *New York Stories* (1989), where Nick Nolte indulges in painterly eurythmics *a la* Jackson Pollock. This is taken further in *Ghost* (1990), where the loft is a space for Patrick Swayze and Demi Moore, after suitable renovations, to express their true artistic selves through the purchasing of wooden sculptures and the throwing of a lot of wet clay. Leslie Felperin, of UK film review magazine *Sight and Sound,* notes that in the re-make of *Great Expectations* (1997), the character of Pip, played by Ethan Hawke, is no longer a lawyer, but an artist living in a loft. In Felperin's words, 'upward mobility, it appears, is no longer seen as being advanced through a profession, but instead via the art gallery'.[12] It is significant in this context that Robert de Niro chose to call his film company Tribeca, possibly after the loft-strewn sector of Manhattan, since film and lofts share a sense of the theatrical moment. Cameramen love lofts, where light and transparency allow the camera much freedom of movement.

As a marketing phenomenon, loft living has, perhaps more than any other lifestyle form, depended on the media for its existence and its frames of reference. 'Image' has been the keystone of the developer's success. But as the lessons and opportunities learned from living in converted industrial spaces gradually filter through broader sections of the housing market, new metaphors and novel representations are bound to emerge.

NOTES

1 _ The exact date when this status changed is unclear, but the city government's Real Estate Board report on loft buildings (1975), offering long-term tax exemption to developers wishing to convert these buildings to residential use, was at this time supported by a barrage of media support for loft living. This said, a 1977 study by the New York City Planning Commission found that 91.5 per cent of all loft conversions in Manhattan were illegal. See Zukin *Loft Living: Culture and Capital in Urban Change* p. 10–11.

2 _ Zukin *op. cit.,* p. 14.

3 _ Zukin *op. cit.,* p. 15.

4 _ As revealed in the 1994 Channel Four documentary 'Art and the CIA' in the series 'Hidden Hands: A Different History of Modernism', written and produced by Frances Stonor Saunders.

5 _ 'A significant factor in the success of the alternative space – as in the success of the galleries that also set up shop there – is that it projects the image of artistic production.' Zukin, *op. cit.,* p. 92.

6 _ The public perception of loft buildings as essentially sites of artistic production rather than just refurbished residential complexes has been the cause of criticisms levelled in San Francisco at Rick Holliday Development Inc., the first business to develop lofts in the mid-1980s for the now-fashionable SoMa (South of Market) area. In response, the company points out that it has included units for use by artists in a number of its loft buildings. ('Real Estate', *San Francisco Examiner,* 17 August 1997).

1 4

1 5

1 3 The 1996 black-and-white Cussons soap advertisement, where a dysfunctional couple occupy a grey minimalist-style loft.

1 4 Ethan Hawke is the character Pip in Alfonso Cuarón's *Great Expectations*, seen here painting in his loft in Manhattan's Astor Place.

1 5 The fabled window-hanging scene between Kevin Klein and John Cleese in the British hit film *A Fish Called Wanda.*

7 _ In conversation with Mark Irving, September 1998. Baker points out that in downtown Atlanta, many loft developments are eligible for tax credits, available to buildings listed on the National Register of Historic Places. Usually, these buildings are earmarked for apartment use and later converted to condominiums after the tax benefit has expired.

8 _ Quotes by Harry Handelsman are taken from a telephone conversation with Mark Irving, September 1998.

9 _ In conversation with Mark Irving, September 1998.

10 _ *The Idler,* 1758–60, p. 40.

11 _ 'Larger Than Life' by Jeremy Myerson, the *Independent on Sunday,* 26 April 1998, p. 58.

12 _ In conversation with Mark Irving, September 1998.

The loft legacy

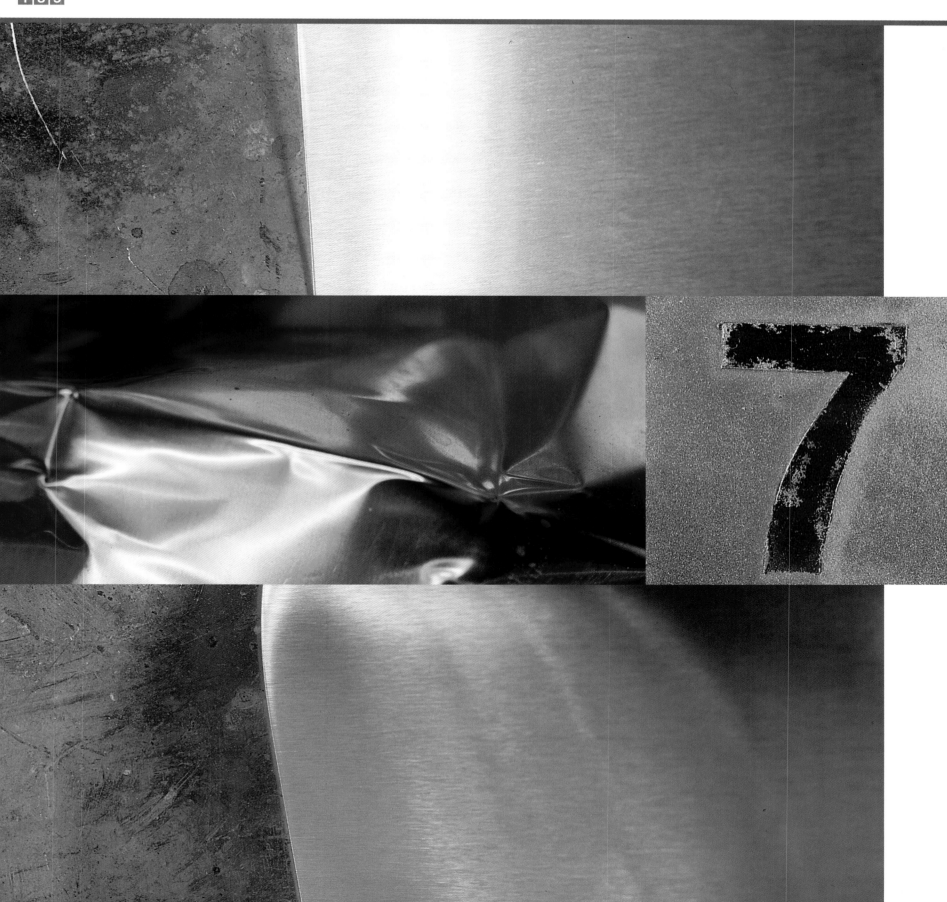

1 Nigel Coates' winning scheme for a suburban estate house, built at the 1998 Ideal Home Exhibition, invokes the open-plan, free-living attributes of the loft. The proposal suggests how the loft form might mutate and move beyond the city.

In the 40 or so years of its history, the loft has shifted from being a space occupied as an economic and socio-political substitute for a conventional domestic environment, to its current perception as a desirable and highly marketable commodity. It has also informed a new approach to the preservation of industrial buildings and the architecture of working within them. For these reasons, the loft now occupies a complex but key position in the world of property and design, as well as in the history of domestic taste. Will it continue to develop and inform domestic and other building types? And what long-term effects will the loft ideal have on our cities?

'The effect of lofts is absolutely real in economic and political terms', says Lee Mallett, former editor of *Estates Times*. Firstly, he argues, it is beginning to have an effect in terms of the way house builders view their product. ('And if ever there was a need for an industry to refresh its product', he comments, 'it's the house-building industry.') The success of developer-led lofts and the media's coverage of their products, suggests Mallett, has led house builders to consider the potential of the inner city as a place to build; of open-plan domestic space as desirable; and of contemporary approaches to architecture as marketable.

The impact of this can already be seen in some newly built apartment blocks, where flats are sold as 'loft like' – usually referring to open-plan spaces, mezzanines and exposed brick walls. More significantly, developers (mostly in cities) are beginning to consider the value once again of houses that are not based on historic styles, but which are contemporary both in their plans and in the way they look.

Although most examples of this trend are by small-scale developers, the building of a contemporary show house at the 1998 Ideal Home Exhibition in London proved that even the noto-riously conservative UK mass-market is beginning to recognize a possible shift in popular taste. The project, called the Oyster House and designed by the architect Nigel Coates, was the winning scheme in the Concept House competition. In describing the ideas behind its flexible open-plan living spaces and contemporary fittings, Coates invoked the free-living values of a loft. The brief for the house was for a suburban setting and the winning scheme illustrates how some principles of loft living could shift beyond the city.

2

2 Situated in a disused tenement house constructed at the end of the nineteenth century, this 130-square-metre (1,400-square-foot) loft-like space was designed for the editor of *Elle* (Czech Republic) magazine in Prague by Olgoj Chorchoj Studio in 1986/7. According to the designers, living in a converted space is the only way for the inhabitants of Prague to live in an 'untypical flat'. However, as most of the old factories and workshops are still in use, 'true' loft spaces are hard to find. Despite not being a former industrial space, the design of this apartment evidently finds its aesthetic in the import of the loft ideal.

Another feature of loft development that interests house builders is the idea of selling shells, leaving the final fitting out of a space to the occupier. 'People will start looking at what happened in lofts and maybe start creating new buildings that have space in them to do as you please', says architect and loft dweller James Soane. 'The trouble is that developers are too greedy and by adding bathrooms and kitchens they get prices that are disproportionate to their real value.'

One of the acknowledged impediments to the building of more experimental domestic architecture is the high price of land. Once these land prices are paid, developers' profit margins are dictated by how cheaply they can make their buildings. As a result, residential developments are usually poorly designed and highly repetitive, responding to economics and perceived ideas of popular taste rather than the particular historic or social context of a site. The market is therefore driven by what developers think people want, rather the initiation of more exciting, challenging possibilities.

However, the success of lofts in the real-estate market (largely during the global recession of the early nineties, which fuelled the loft movement by lowering the price of former commercial buildings) is significant in that it has shown that more experimental forms of domestic development can also be profitable. While new, contemporary forms may take some time to filter down to the speculative house-building market, there are already new-build apartment projects where loft principles are being tested. As part of the Homes for the Future project in Glasgow, for example, the Burrell Company is building a new development of shell units – designed by Ushida Findlay Architects – where the fit-out will be left to the occupier. As architect Kathryn Findlay says: 'It helps the developer because there is less capital outlay and it is good for the buyer because there is more flexibility in the plan.'

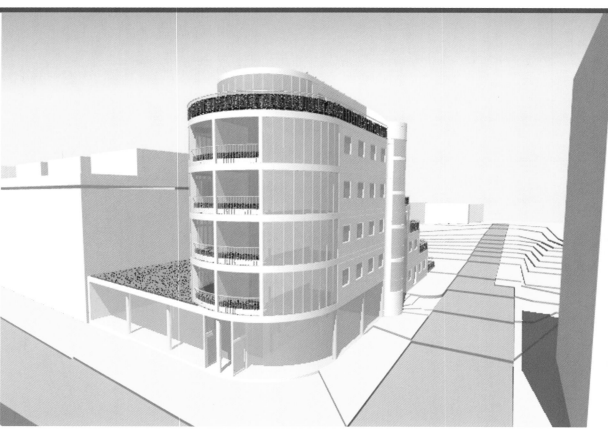

5

3 **4** This new subsidized housing development in Glasgow, completed in 1999 by architects Ushida Findlay, draws on loft culture in the way that the units are sold as shells, leaving the final fit out to the occupier.

5 **6** **7** 'New Loft', a scheme completed in 1999 in Cologne, Germany, and designed by Brandlhuber & Kniess + Partner draws on loft culture both in the way it is marketed to appeal to a fashionable clientele, as well as in its design. The irregular plans and sections of the new-build structure are intended to make each of the 12 apartments individual, while the final fit out of the shell units is again left to the occupier. According to the architects, the building, without a former purpose, 'is more simplified' than the lofts from which it draws inspiration.

3

4

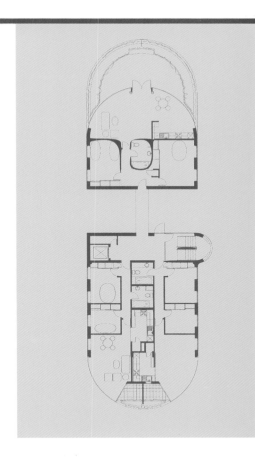

6

7

In New York, loft dweller and professor of architecture Diane Lewis agrees that what she calls the 'long span' quality of lofts is the future of domestic space. She is currently working on a project for a client in up-town New York, not traditionally a loft district, where the walls of a conventional apartment are being removed to create an open-plan space 15 x 6 metres (50 x 20 feet). For Lewis, the postmodern return to conventional domestic forms in the eighties was just a blip in the much larger modernist programme. 'I've proved in my work that the free plan is where we're heading', she says. By 'free plan', she is clear to point out, she doesn't just mean minimalist, which is what she describes as 'a visual style', but rather *la void*, the volumetrically generous space described in a lecture by the legendary French designer Charlotte Perriand as one of the great accomplishments of the twentieth century. In that void, says Lewis, the occupier is given the space to dream.

This idea that the legacy of the loft is in some ways a continuation of the modernist programme is echoed by London architect and loft dweller Paul Monaghan. 'What has become the loft aesthetic', he says, 'is the modernism that we all know. What it allowed architects to bring back is the idea of open-plan living. That's down to *Elle Decoration* magazine and the Sunday supplements.' Now that this popularizing of contemporary living has taken hold, argues Monaghan, there is the potential for other new forms of building and urban planning to progress. 'If people allow it in their houses', he says, 'they will allow it anywhere.'

8

8   9 Loft living is clearly one of the ins
the London apartment of the architect J
Completed in 1989, the structure of the
in London's Hammersmith draws
magnifies, the aesthetics of industria
typically colonized by loft dwellers. Ir
open-plan spaces, expanses of glazing
expressed structure articulate the traditi
the Modern Movement and loft culture.

While it might be difficult to prove a direct lineage between lofts and some of the world's most dynamic new architecture, an approach to working in the shells of existing buildings – and even the forms of some new buildings – have certainly been informed by the design and culture of lofts.

From the earliest days, the association between the artist and the loft has informed an approach to the design of both commercial and public galleries. In New York, the galleries of SoHo and Chelsea are often treated with a loft aesthetic, occupying former industrial buildings and even leaving intact original fittings and other signs of the building's former use. But even at a larger, public scale, new galleries draw – wittingly or unwittingly – on loft culture. In well-known examples in Paris at the Musée d'Orsay and in Berlin at the Hamburger Hof, former railway stations have been converted to show art. Meanwhile, in London the defunct Bankside Power Station is being adapted by Herzog & de Meuron to create the new Tate Gallery of Modern Art. When it opens in 2000 the gallery will – with its giant winches and industrial detritus still intact, juxtaposed with its calm, naturally lit gallery spaces – look like the largest loft in the world.

1 1

1 0 **1 1** Since artists began occupying lofts in New York in the 1950s, defunct industrial buildings have become the preferred environment for the display of art. Projects in this lineage range from small private galleries to vast public institutions like the German Design Centre in Essen, by Norman Foster and Partners, and the new Tate Gallery of Modern Art at Bankside, London by Herzog & de Meuron, which opens in 2000.

Despite the mini boom created for architects by the fitting out of lofts, there is a frustration in the design profession that work should not always take place in the shells of existing buildings. There must, architects argue, still be room for new building in the city. Piers Gough, a partner at CZWG and architect for a number of loft developments for the Manhattan Loft Corporation, says, 'for architects, developing old buildings is like having a vegetarian meal when you're a meat eater: its OK, quite tasty at the time, but afterwards you feel hungry.'[1]

There are, however, some brand-new buildings that are also informed by the loft aesthetic. In some cases, their raw contemporary appearance has been made acceptable to people because of their familiarity with the loft look. In the Netherlands for example, the concrete interior of the VPRO office building by architects MVRDV is presented and furnished like a loft, while the large, void-like spaces of new-build galleries like London's Lisson Gallery by Tony Fretton and the Walsall Art Gallery by Caruso St John, bear some comparison with the volumes and finishes of lofts. In a growing quantity of newly built houses too, the loft lifestyle has clearly informed the decision for open-plan space and bare, natural finishes.

1 2 **1 3** **1 4** In Queens, New York, the PS1 Institute for Contemporary Art by Frederick Fisher (refurbished in 1997) is converted from a nineteenth-century school building. Its raw, peeled-back interiors and cut-up volumes provide spaces for installations and artworks, and recall the rough environment of early SoHo lofts.

1 4

1 5 Despite their subversive nature, lofts are rendered acceptable to the establishment because of the patina of age provided by the host buildings. Architects have learned from this and new interventions for major projects, like these live/work lofts in San Francisco – called the Oriental Warehouse – by Fisher Friedman Associates (completed between 1988 and 1994). The new insertion is a steel-frame structure set back from the existing 'showcase' brick walls of an 1868 bonded warehouse.

1 6 Now that the converted industrial building has become the preferred workplace for creative industries, even new buildings for this purpose draw on the loft model for inspiration. In the Netherlands, offices for the VPRO television production company by the architects MVRDV (completed in 1997) illustrates this with its raw concrete aesthetic and open, irregular plan.

Most obviously though, the architectural treatment of lofts has had an impact on the shops, cafés, bars and other leisure buildings frequented by the fashionable urban middle classes on both sides of the Atlantic. Shops like the delicatessen Dean & De Luca in New York, the Aveda cosmetics store in London's Marylebone, the SCP furniture showroom in Shoreditch and a number of furniture stores in Manhattan's SoHo clearly owe a debt to lofts. The same goes for numerous fashionable bars, clubs and cafés of cities like Berlin, Glasgow, Manchester and San Francisco where the materials, fittings and gritty realism are akin to those of the classic loft. Even the contemporary office has taken on some of the attributes of the loft. Large free-plan spaces carved out of old industrial buildings have been found to function just as well for group work as they do for living. As a result, the loft aesthetic of oversized furniture, stripped floors and industrial fittings is now making an appearance in media-related businesses such as advertising, design and television production.

17 The loft has become such a universal model for the bohemian domestic environment that even when such a project is newly built, it is planned to resemble a converted industrial space. This graphic design and photography studio and home, designed by Tanner Leddy Maytum Stacy Architects in 1991 for Thomas Heinser and Madeleine Corson, is constructed in an alley in the South of Market area of San Francisco using maintenance-free industrial materials.

18 Similarly, the creative working environment draws on the large volumes and use of natural lighting associated with lofts. Here, the Milan office of the architect Mario Bellini – formerly a foundry, converted between 1990 and 1993 – preserves the building's industrial ethos.

19 In the sixties and seventies, the diverse and dynamic loft movement in New York and Berlin, as illustrated here with a postcard by Dieter Kramer of Kreuzberg graffiti, was partly about protest at the threatened demolition of former industrial districts. Now these same districts are threatened with becoming sanitized ghettoes for the affluent middle class.

20 The SCP furniture showroom in London's Shoreditch area, designed by Munkenbeck and Marshall in 1998, is an example of a transformation of a former industrial building into a retail space.

But while this more enlightened attitude to contemporary design might improve our towns and cities, other effects of the loft movement might not be so desirable. In the Kreuzberg district of Berlin, says artist and loft dweller Dieter Kramer, the commercialization of lofts has killed the bohemian nature of the district and turned it into a chic, but less interesting place. 'There are very few bohemian lofts now', says Kramer. 'Before the fall of the Wall, Kreuzberg was neglected and not valuable. Now it is the centre of the city. Prices have gone up. Lofts are now DM5,000 a square metre when they used to DM1,000. You used to have to buy a whole building if you wanted a loft; now they sell them in little parts. That is absolutely new in Berlin.' The result, says Kramer, is that 'people have now gone to the old, rotten quarters of the former East Berlin. Artists always go to a quarter where it is cheap and neglected. Then come the richer people.'

In New York too, architect and loft dweller Henry Smith-Miller complains about the changes that have occurred in SoHo since he first moved there in the early seventies. 'It has turned into a great big mall', he says. 'All the people from the north east – we call them the "bridge and tunnel" crowd – come here to stroll around and see all the "crazy artists". Now all the galleries have moved to the West 20s because they don't want the petite bourgeoisie wandering around. Instead, we have smart, fashionable hotels here – the Soho Grand and the Mercer.' As a result, says Smith-Miller, loft living, in New York at least, may have lost some of its meaning. 'It will probably become terribly boring. Lofts have no indeterminate qualities anymore, no excitement. There is no more subversive behaviour.'

William Menking, a tutor in history and theory at the Pratt Institute in New York and a Tribeca loft dweller since 1978, has developed a thesis suggesting that what we are actually seeing in places like his district and SoHo is the surburbanization of the city. 'My neighbourhood has been transformed into Triburbia', he writes, 'a district increasingly as suburban as any of the 100-mile metropolitan ring around New York City. In its transformation to an affluent residential suburb, much of the dynamic urban life of the area has been lost.' He points out that lofts are central to this transformation. 'Their large size – [280–380 square-metres] 3–4,000 square-feet is common – allows families to stay in the city and yet live as if in a family-centred suburb.'[2]

But, argues Lee Mallett, this sort of change in a district is all part of the free economic and social changes that are natural in a city. Of the loft districts of London he says, 'All those inner-city areas are controlled by Labour councils who traditionally supply work and housing to the community. They want to preserve the existing political and social situation – to resist gentrification – so that they stay in power. But they are realizing that to persuade the woolly mammoths to come back is unrealistic. The London boroughs of Hackney and Islington have changed tune and allowed the natural economic process to take place.' For Mallett, the freedom of movement, exchange and use in the city that lofts typify is the way forward. 'In the "new media" inner city', he says, 'planners should allow people to use buildings for whatever purpose they want. If you allow them to switch it will work. That's the job of a local authority.'

So has this gentrification and commercialization of the loft movement destroyed its culture and devalued its contribution to saving industrial urban heritage? 'Clerkenwell has already been taken over by suits', says Joe Kerr, senior tutor in history and theory at the Royal College of Art in London. 'And nobody who is not a stock dealer can afford to live in Manhattan. The wages of the few distort the value of property for the many', he argues. As a result, says Kerr, the artists and colonies of cheaper buildings move on, in New York to DUMBO (Down Under the Manhattan Bridge), or in London to Bermondsey or the outer reaches of east London.

But, Kerr points out, the positive effects of the recolonization of the centres of cities like Berlin, New York and London far outweigh the negative. 'The thing I find incredibly exciting about it is to see people moving back into the centre of the city. Whoever they are', he says. With this movement of middle classes, he argues, comes better services for everyone, including education and leisure. He has a word of warning though, and that is that the international homogeneity of loft space – the phenomenon of 'Manhattan-style lofts' whether in Berlin, Chicago, London, New Orleans or New York – should be resisted if its spirit of individuality is to survive.

 Developers and estate agents are quick to capitalize on the rise in value of districts when loft dwellers move in. Clerkenwell Central is a homogeneous-looking residential development comprising warehouse 'apartments' situated in the shell of former newspaper distribution buildings, as well as new-build town houses with double-height living spaces.

21

This warning is particularly pertinent in the light of the recent unveiling of a new room-set at the Geffrye Museum, London's famous museum of domestic taste. Intended to represent the style of the 1990s, the set is designed to reflect the archetypal loft. Now that the loft has become the subject of museum displays and history books, does this signify its death – at least in the UK and US? And will it launch its birth – as we have begun to see – in countries throughout Europe and the rest of the world?

'Loft development is led by commercial factors', says Manhattan Loft Corporation chairman Harry Handelsman. 'Now there's a strong demand for commercial space again in London. The market for lofts is subject to the regular market. People buy lofts for all the same reasons they buy other property: for living and for investment. We will see a tail-off, but it's something that will always sit alongside general residential.'

That's the commercial line. But the loft, as this book shows, is so much more than a commodity. It is about attitudes to lifestyle, politics and architecture. It is also about social change and cities. But most importantly, perhaps, it is about freedom, experimentation and progression. The loft may have become a museum exhibit, but its legacy lives on.

2|2 The stereotype loft interior of the 1990s, with its new wood floor, designer furniture and accompanying lifestyle connotations (note the inclusion of the glossy *Wallpaper** magazine) has recently become the subject of a permanent display on post-war domestic taste at the Geffrye Museum in London. The image is a far cry from the politically motivated, raw aesthetic of early lofts. Away from this compromised commodity, however, the real loft-dweller's attitude survives in spacious, low-rent or squatted former industrial spaces throughout the world.

NOTES

1 _ Piers Gough in conversation with Alicia Pivaro for 'Loft Squared', an exhibition at the RIBA Architecture Centre, September/October 1995.

2 _ 'From Tribeca to Triburbia: a new concept of the city' in *The Unknown City: Contesting Architecture and Social Space*, eds Iain Borden, Joe Kerr, Alicia Pivaro and Jane Rendell (forthcoming).

Designers' contact details

Miki Astori

Via Cesare 7, 20123 Milan, Italy

Tel: 02 89 40 42 51

Fax: 02 89 42 86 52

Felicity Bell

Unit 6, 63–67 Rosoman Street, London EC1R 0HY, UK

Tel: 171 689 0213

Fax: 171 713 6759

Fernando Campana

rua Baráo de Tatui, 219 cep, 012 26030 São Paulo, SP Brazil

Tel/Fax: 55 11 825 3408

Cristian Cirici & Carlos Bassó

c. Pujades 63 2n, 08005 Barcelona, Spain

Tel: 85 47 52

Fax: 09 67 48

e-mail: ciricibasso@coac.cs

Dean/Wolf Architects

40 Hudson Street, New York, NY 10013, USA

Tel/Fax: 212 732 1887

e-mail: deanwolf1@aol.com

de Metz Green Architects

Unit 4, 250 Finchley Road, London NW3 6DN, UK

Tel: 171 435 1144

Fax: 171 435 0884

e-mail: demetz.co.uk

Ernst & Niklaus Architekten ETH/SIA

Bahnhofstrasse 102, CH-5000 Aarau, Switzerland

Tel: 62 823 78 68

Fax: 62 823 78 89

e-mail: en.arch@echo.ch

Form Werkstatt

Anglerstrasse 6, 80339 Munich, Germany

Tel: 89 540 70023

Fax: 89 540 70124

e-mail: siggi.pfundt@t-online.de

Michael H. Green of Green Homan

78 Greys Hill, Henley-on-Thames, Oxon RG9 1SL, UK

Tel: 01491 578197

Fax: 01491 413911

Mark Guard Architects

161 Whitfield Street, London W1P 5RY, UK

Tel: 171 380 1199

Fax: 171 387 5441

e-mail: mga@markguard.co.uk

Hardy Holzman Pfeiffer Associates

902 Broadway, New York, NY 10010, USA

Tel: 212 677 6030

Fax: 212 979 0535

e-mail: dwaters@hhpa.com

Joachim Hesse + Partner GmbH

Kurfürstendamm 103/4, 10711 Berlin, Germany

Tel: 30 893 605 20

Fax: 30 893 605 55

e-mail: JoHesse@compuserve.com

Kramer Ausstellungsbau

Schlesische Strasse 26, 10997 Berlin-Kreuzberg, Germany

Tel/Fax: 30 611 6454

Diane Lewis Architect

34 West Ninth Street No. 4, New York, NY 10011, USA

Tel: 212 388 0094

Fax: 212 388 0547

LOT/EK Architecture

55 Little West 12th Street, New York, NY 10014, USA

Tel/Fax: 212 255 9326

e-mail: lotekarch@aol.com

Rick Mather Architects

123 Camden High Street, London NW1 7UR, UK

Tel: 171 284 1727

Fax: 171 267 7826

e-mail: rma@mather.demon.co.uk

Matteo Piazza (fotografo)

Corso di Porta Ticinese 69, 20123 Milan, Italy

Tel: 02 58 10 65 64

Fax: 02 58 10 69 26

Mark Pimlott

49/59 Old Street, London EC1V 9DA, UK

Tel: 171 336 0310

Fax: 171 600 1092

e-mail: markpimlott@hotmail.com

Project Orange

Unit Seven, 74–84 Banner Street, London EC1Y 8JU, UK

Tel/Fax: 171 336 8941

Resolution 4: Architecture

150 West 28th Street, Suite 1902, New York, NY 10001, USA

Tel: 212 675 9266

Fax: 212 206 0944

e-mail: jtanney@re4A.com

Ken Rorrison Architects

c/o Buschow Henley, 21 Little Portland Street, London W1N 5AF, UK

Tel: 171 580 2899

Fax: 171 580 2866

e-mail: studio@bharch.demon.co.uk

Alain Salomon Architecte d.u.c.

2 rue Frochot, 75009 Paris, France

Tel: 1 42 82 09 88

Fax: 1 42 80 41 97

e-mail: AlainSalomon@compuserve.com

Smith-Miller + Hawkinson Architects

305 Canal Street, New York, NY 10013, USA

Tel: 212 966 3875

Fax: 212 966 3877

e-mail: taylor@smharch.com

Marja Sopanen & Olli Sarlin

Uudenmaankatu 26, 00120 Helsinki, Finland

Tel/Fax: 358 9 611 551

Els Staal, Interior Architect

16 rue du Faubourg Saint Denis, 75010 Paris, France

Tel/Fax: 1 42 46 22 67

Tankard Bowkett

First Floor, 8 Nile Street, London N1 7R5, UK

Tel: 171 251 3597

Fax: 171 251 6880

24/seven architecture & design

Studio 3, 16 Anning Street, London EC2A 3HB, UK

Tel/Fax: 171 684 8138

e-mail: twentyfour.seven@virgin.net

Wells Mackereth Architects

10 Archer Street, London W1, UK

Tel: 171 287 5504

Fax: 171 287 5506

e-mail: wellsmackereth@btinternet.com

Willingale Associates

Architects and Development Consultants

60–62 Clerkenwell Road, London EC1M 5PX, UK

Tel/Fax: 171 490 5506

e-mail: arch@bluebase.com

Index of designers and projects

Published 1999 by Gingko Press Inc.

5768 Paradise Drive, Suite J

Corte Madera, CA 94925, USA

e-mail: gingko@linex.com

and

Gingko Press Verlag GmbH

Hamburger Strasse 180

D-22083 Hamburg, Germany

e-mail: gingkopress@t-online.de

Published by arrangement with Laurence King Publishing

Copyright © 1999 Calmann & King Ltd.

This book was designed and produced by Calmann & King Ltd., London

A catalogue record for this book is available from the British Library.

ISBN 3-927258-83-0

Design: Paul Cohen at the north terminal

Chapter opener photography: Andrew Penketh

Coordinating Researcher: Jennifer Hudson

Printed in Singapore